How to Sell Your Mid-Size Business

Maximize Price with Marketing and Bidding

Ney Grant

Graeme Plant, Editor
Don Krier, Editor
Mandy Cuda, Editor

A special thanks to Graeme for the great deal of time he spent cleaning up my blog-style writing. He also added a few "Deal Extracts" (personal war stories) that help liven up the book.

Legal Disclaimers and End User Rights

Table of Contents

Introduction   **1**

DataPack Offer   2

Preparing Your Company and Knowing When to Sell   **3**

Knowing when to sell: Where are you on the life-cycle curve?   4

Timing the sale of a business   7

Burned Out?   8

How long does it take to sell a business?   9

Example deal timeline   10

Selling your business within two years?   11

Two business owners, two different approaches to business   13

The emotional roller coaster of selling your business   14

Eight common mistakes business sellers make   17

Creating your dream team of professionals   20

Marketing the Business   **23**

Marketing = Competitive Bidding = Maximum Selling Price   23

The Competitive Bidding Process   26

Negotiations   34

International Marketing   34

Earnings: EBITDA   **37**

Adjusting earnings – Add-backs   39

The Essence of Business Valuation   **45**

Future earnings equal value 46

Why use Multiples of Earnings 48

Multiples of EBITDA 48

Middle Market Business Valuation **49**

Valuation guide and chart 49

Value premium for "quality" businesses 51

Return on investment 55

Confidentiality **59**

How do you market a company and keep it confidential? 60

Should you tell your employees? 61

Business brokers to Investment Bankers: Fees and Services **63**

Business brokerage 64

Merger & Acquisition Firms 65

Broker and advisor regulations and licensing 66

Commissions and fees 67

We have a buyer for your business! (Not) 70

Business-for-sale seminars 71

Choosing a business broker / M & A advisor 72

Broker/advisors do more than find a buyer 74

Taxes and Deal Structuring **77**

Ordinary income vs. capital gains 78

Deferring taxes 80

The letter of intent explained 82

Earn-outs **85**

What are earn-outs?	86
Business are bought for future earnings	86
Scenario 1 – stable earnings	*87*
Scenario 2 – supported growth	*88*
Scenario 3 – unsupported growth	*90*
Scenario 4 – recession-proofing a transaction	*90*
How often are earn-outs used?	91
Earn-out period	92
Amounts in earn-outs	92
Controls and restrictions	93
Strategic vs. Financial Buyers	**95**
Strategic buyers	96
Financial buyers and private equity groups	97
Typical middle market PE – committed funds	98
Typical lower middle market PE – search funds	98
Why private equity uses debt to leverage its investment	99
Due Diligence and Getting to the Finish Line	**103**
What is appropriate due diligence?	104
How not to do due diligence	105
Other due diligence issues	106
Paper or Electronic Deal Room?	106
In the end, there must be some degree of trust	107
Closing a deal: Moving from negotiations to logistics	109
Purchase Agreements	**110**
Sample Purchase Agreements – Datapack	110

A Tale of Two Deals   111

The asset sale vs. the stock sale   111

The strategic buyer vs. the financial buyer   115

Deal structuring and getting what you want   118

Deal attorneys   121

Life as an M & A advisor and Deal-Maker   123

Landing engagements and selling your services   123

Meeting with business owners   124

Buyer/seller meetings: Smoke jumping   127

Flying south   131

Exciting times: Meeting walkouts   135

Mundane tasks – Doing what it takes   136

Negotiations   137

Closing the deal   139

Appendix   141

Tale of Two Deals: The Private Equity Letter of Intent   141

Tale of Two Deals: Strategic Buyer Letter of Intent   149

Tale of Two Deals: Due Diligence Request List   153

101 Things You Should Know About Selling Your Business 165

Introduction

Welcome to the definitive guide to selling your mid-sized business. We have condensed years of experience preparing, marketing and selling businesses into this book. I've written many hundreds of blog entries, spoken at seminars, made hundreds of presentation, toured and met hundreds of business owners across the country and continents. We have offered volumes of advice and information on this topic, but this is intended to be a comprehensive guide to what can be a prickly process. We're hoping you'll walk away from this book smarter, more confident and readier than ever to embark on this next step of your life.

Happy selling.

Ney Grant

ney@woodbridgegrp.com

Deal Extracts

Many chapters include first-hand stories about buyers and sellers we have encountered. Some of these deals closed, and some didn't. These are stories of integrity and greed. Some are useful and educational, and some are just plain entertaining. In deal-making, as with other parts of life, reality can be much stranger than fiction.

DataPack Offer

I have assembled some files and documents that go along with the book and these will be sent to you by emailing me at ney@woodbridgegrp.com. The Datapack includes:

- The final deal agreements for the "Tale of Two Deals" examples used in the book. One is a Stock Purchase Agreement and the other is an Asset Purchase Agreement.

- The due diligence request list included in the book is fairly brief. I've included in the datapack a more detailed request list.

- I have included two deal modeling spreadsheets actually used by buyers. One is from a large strategic buyer and one is from a financial private equity buyer. It is interesting to see how buyers view an acquisition from their point of view.

Preparing Your Company and Knowing When to Sell

You may be thinking about selling your business now or in the next few years. Timing can be important, not only in regard to the economic climate, but also in terms of the life cycle of your business.

Deal Extracts

An Example of Good Timing…

We had a client in 2008/09 (in the middle of the deepest recession since the great depression) whose alternative energy business was growing rapidly. At the same time, a new President came into office with a major focus on alternative energy. Amid all that optimism, it was extremely difficult to nail down how much growth this company would experience. An unsolicited offer came in for about six times earnings before interest, taxes, depreciation, and amortization (EBITDA). After creating some competition by getting another buyer interested, the bidding exceeded 12 times EBITDA. Could the owner have kept it and grown the company himself to realize an even bigger gain? Quite possibly, but it was a great exit for the seller and there was significant risk in many of the projects that could have slowed the revenue growth.

… And Bad Timing

In 2007, we provided an opinion of value of around $7 million to a husband and wife team that owned a steel fabrication company that provided product to *a number of companies, none of which were more than 15 percent of their business. The husband wanted to sell, but his wife wanted to gross $10 million minimum on the sale. She convinced her husband that if they waited just a few more years and grew earnings a bit more, they could get more money for the business. Unfortunately, though their customer base was diverse, almost all were suppliers to RV manufacturers. Gas prices suddenly spiked to $4 per gallon and the RV industry went off a cliff. In 2008, the company declared bankruptcy and closed its doors.*

Knowing when to sell: Where are you on the life-cycle curve?

There are many reasons that business owners sell their companies. Three common ones are:

- Retirement age is nearing

- New skill sets are required to reach a higher level of financial performance (I'm not good at delegating and I can't work 37 hours per day)

- Burnout (If I hear one more employee complaint!!!)

Others reasons for putting your business up include health issues, partner disagreements or a desire to pursue new opportunities.

It is easy to chart out when to sell, but much harder in reality to know where you are in the business life cycle. Many M & A firm websites feature bell curve charts that illustrate the best time in a business life cycle to sell. Here is the typical chart:

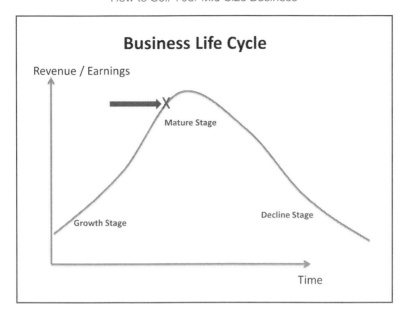

That looks nice, and it looks pretty easy to see when to sell. It's right at the red "X.", correct?

However, I've never actually seen a business with that particular curve. In many cases, they look more like this:

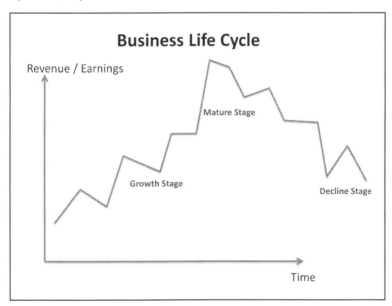

But those constant fluctuations in growth, decline and maturity aren't the only factors that will have your bell curve looking like a mountain range. The biggest issue is that you can't see the future. So, actually, most curves look like the chart on the following page.

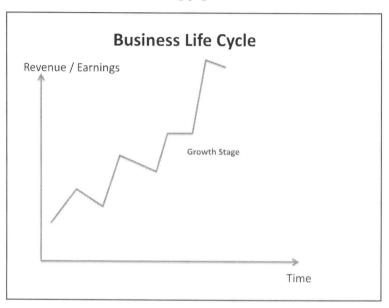

Now it's a bit harder to see where to sell. Is that last little dip down the beginning of a long decline, or just the kind of hiccup that any business experiences from time to time? And then there are the external issues that can kill a business, as the spike in gas price did to the steel company, or the 9-11 terrorist attacks did to the travel industry in 2001.

Externalities aside, some business owners are far better at identifying where that red X goes than others. It mostly has to do with understanding your company and market. I see a surprising number of owners who are not in touch with how their business is doing. Sometimes it stems from a simple lack of accounting controls. Other times, the owner is burned out and spending less time in the office, which can also make him or her less aware of how the business is doing.

I sometimes can see a decline coming, and will gently try to guide an owner to that understanding. I never want to push the issue too hard, for fear of a perceived conflict of interest in trying to push a sale that will increase my income. So I advise and stand back. Sometimes, unfortunately, I watch the company slip into an un-sellable condition. Once a company reaches apparent decline, they are almost impossible to sell at any price. . While it may sound self-serving the biggest mistake many business owners make is waiting too long before they sell.

Timing the sale of a business

You can accidentally work years for essentially no pay if you ignore obvious signs that it is time to sell your company. In some ways, timing the sale of your business is like trying to time when to buy and sell a stock. Although it can be hard to guess which market trends will affect your business, sometimes it can be obvious. I remember two business owners who contacted me about their respective companies. Both had serious health problems. They had each waited too long to sell and the businesses had declined. I tried to help and, in both cases, I failed to sell the business. It was a lesson for me, because I spent a lot of time working on those engagements. Not only did I not make any money, but I wasn't able to help the clients.

Even if the owners' respective illnesses led to the decline of their businesses, buyers wondered if there was an inherent problem beyond anyone's control. For me as an intermediary, there is only the risk of spending a lot of time on a deal and not making any money. But prospective buyers are often putting their entire life savings at risk. So they see a decline in business that is **probably** due to the owner's illness, but might not be, and they get nervous. What if the decline has nothing to do with owner's health and they're putting their savings into a sinking ship that they can't right? The buyers we found weren't willing to take that risk.

Those were painful episodes, but these owners should have sold before letting their companies decline. I get a lot of calls from owners who watched their companies slide for years. Often, there isn't much we can do. A business owner who hangs onto his or her business too long often loses far more value from the business than they make in salary during that time. You can think of this as "working for free."

Say a business is making $2,000,000 in earnings per year, and the enterprise value multiple is five times the earnings at that point in time, so the value is about $10 million. The owner burns out, starts going on extended trips and isn't paying attention to the company. Within three years, earnings decline to $1,200,000 and he decides to sell. He took out about five million during those three years, but the company is now worth about four times (or even less), or about $5,000,000. Multiples are lower for lower earnings, especially ones in decline. He just worked three years for nothing. In fact, the company may be un-sellable now, because it is exceedingly difficult to convince buyers that simple "burnout" is the main reason for a decline, although it often is.

Timing the sale to hit the company's peak value is always hard, so it is best to watch for signs of trouble and act accordingly. It's always better to sell a little early than too late. There is a saying on Wall Street that bulls make money and bears make money, but pigs get eaten. Getting greedy and trying to time your sale to squeeze as much money out of your business as possible could have a bad result.

Burned Out?

Often new ownership can interrupt the business life cycle curve and breathe new growth into a company. I received a thank you call the other day from a seller who, after 4 years, had received his final payment on the note he was carrying when he sold his business (always nice to hear). He said he was glad he sold his business when he did, and that the two guys that took over and managed the business after he sold it had created a new market and had grown the company substantially.

Unfortunately, as I've mentioned before, it is hard to get paid for that future growth if the company isn't on a clear upward path. If the company is on a clear growth path, it is often quite possible to set up a performance based compensation called an earnout. I've written an entire chapter on earnouts later in this book.

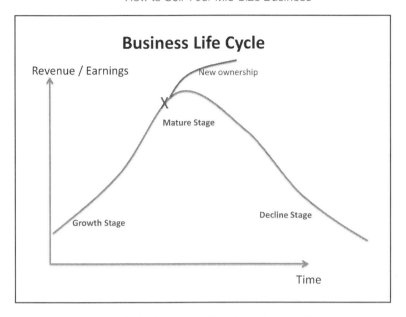

How long does it take to sell a business?

This depends on the complexity of the business, financing required, and a variety of other factors. Since our practice focuses on medium-sized businesses, I rarely see deals close in less than six months.

We once "pre-sold" a company because we had identified a buyer who clearly wanted it. We still needed to do the financial analysis and opinion of value, which would normally take a few weeks. In this case, it took longer because the books were not in ideal shape. We wanted to make sure the seller got the best price, so we made sure we ran our normal marketing process to attract additional buyers. Although we did attract other interest, the original buyer made a strong offer and it was negotiated and accepted within a few weeks. The buyer needed some financing for this eight million dollar deal. I was convinced that the earnings and cash flow were valid. The buyer was convinced, and the seller was living proof with his extravagant lifestyle supported by the business. Convincing the bankers was far more difficult, and it took six months to find a lender that would finance the deal.

We have found that the average selling time is nine months from start to close for medium-sized companies. For companies, the average is closer to six months for a good-performing company without complexities like those I described above. If the business owner has unrealistic expectations, the business can sit on the market for a long time

Example deal timeline

Day one

Dave filled out a form from our website. We called him back, and he answered from the golf course. He said he wanted to wait until after the first of the year to talk.

At two months

I called Dave, and he wanted to wait until February.

At three months

Dave was interested in talking about selling his business, so we requested financials to provide an opinion of value. It took a few weeks, and then there was an issue of cash vs. accrual accounting. Dave's company was growing and using cash accounting up until two years prior. To give a good opinion of value, we needed a good estimate of earnings using accrual accounting, which took time.

At four months

We met with Dave, presented our analysis and provided a company presentation of our process and he tentatively agreed to an engagement, pending his calls to check our references.

At five months

After preparing a complete financial summary, book, and other materials, we began our marketing campaign. The campaign targeted financial buyers (private equity) and a list of strategic buyers.

At six months

A number of buyers, both strategic and private equity, signed confidentiality agreements. We received eight indications of interest (first round bids) and completed four site visits and management (buyer/seller) meetings. We then got two letters of intent, and selected a strategic buyer.

This buyer was the CEO of a larger competing organization, who went out on his own with help of an SBA loan.

At seven months

During due diligence it became clear that the buyer was a perfect candidate to buy and run the company, but financing the deal would be a challenge.

At eight months

The buyer was approved for $6 million dollars in Small Business Administration loans, larger than normal because of a special program for manufacturing firms. The SBA process was started.

At 10 months

The SBA process ended, badly. The bank's chairman personally killed the loan at the last minute (after being approved by underwriting) because he had previously seen the bank get burned by the same kind of business.

At 11 months

Dave wanted to find a different buyer — maybe one with more available cash so we could avoid the SBA process. We countered that this was an excellent buyer and that we should help him get financing. We started the long SBA process again with a new bank.

At 12 months

The SBA loan came through. After more than a year of work, we got the deal closed. The seller had been waiting to fly to Hawaii with his family, and within a week, he was gone on vacation. The buyer moved and immediately established some new out-state business and was happily running his new company.

Selling your business within two years?

If you are contemplating selling your business within the next two years, it pays to start thinking about your tax strategy. It's simple in theory. You pay a percentage of your earnings in taxes. But when you sell your company, you get paid a multiple of the earnings as a selling price. Often, the price is at least four to six times earnings. So, though you normally want to minimize taxes, in the year or two before you sell, you don't want to do that. You want to maximize earnings for a bigger basis used with the multiple.

Here is an example. Typically, you categorize purchases as expenses, even if your accountant is telling you that you should capitalize and expense over time as depreciation. This minimizes earnings and minimizes the resulting taxes. In a sale, the earnings used are EBITDA. Depreciation doesn't count – it gets added back into earnings by definition. In the year or two before you sell, you want to purchase as much, say, tools and software as you can and capitalize/depreciate those.

Inventory is another area you need to think about. There are two official methods to valuing inventory – FIFO (First In, First Out) and LIFO (Last In, First Out). In this business we like to say that some owners use a third method: WIFL (Whatever I Feel Like). If you are going to use WIFL, keep in mind that it is well worth paying a few dollars more in taxes to gain a multiple of those earnings when you sell.

Then there are personal expenses written off as business expenses. We see everything from owners expensing a personal car to owners using a company work crew to build a vacation home. We can adjust earnings to show that they are actually higher than what the bottom line suggests. However, there are limits to what some buyers will accept. Too many adjustments will make some buyers nervous and, often, the adjustments become a negotiated item. From the buyer's perspective, the risk goes up and the value goes down. Financing gets harder, adjustments get thrown out and trust issues often pop up between the buyer and seller. It's far better to just come clean and pay the taxes in the year or two prior to selling (well, not completely clean – everyone seems to write off **some** personal expenses and that is an accepted practice).

I don't like to get into a situation where the business owner wishes he or she had done some things differently in the years prior (though this happens fairly often). It's a shame, because I know they could have sold the business for more if only they implemented a few of these simple steps.

A good mergers and acquisitions advisor will work with you for a year or two before you sell. They will review your year-end statements and identify areas where you can increase the value of your business without much effort. Or, they can identify problem areas (such as too much inventory) that you can work on so it isn't a last-minute crisis. I have clients right now whom I've been working with for more than two years. Most of us in this industry are patient. It's better to sell a good clean business in two years than try to force a sale of a messy business today.

Recently, I ran into two scenarios that initially seemed similar. They both involved owners who wished to sell their middle-market businesses and exit the business after about a year. Other than that, they couldn't have been more different. One owner had looked ahead and was prepared for the sale. The other hadn't.

Two business owners, two different approaches to business

First, let's talk about the prepared company. "Let me put it to you this way," the owner said. "I took a six-week European vacation this summer and the company hardly missed me. I knew I wanted to sell in the next five to 10 years, so I hired a general manager four years ago, and he pretty much runs the place."

That says a lot right there. Prospective buyers love knowing that the very existence of the business doesn't hang on one person. It becomes obvious when the owner can sit through a meeting with us and not be interrupted multiple times. I can't emphasize this enough – buyers are extremely sensitive to business owners who haven't given up any control, yet want to sell and leave.

Money is a big obstacle to weaning these owners off their businesses. Many of them remember the days when the only way to make ends meet was to do almost everything themselves. Even when the company gets larger and can be self-sustaining, it is hard to "waste" money on hiring an expensive manager when you can do it yourself. But when you are thinking about selling, it actually makes more financial sense to get the manager and build the proper team. If you can show that the company doesn't need you, then you can adjust the earnings ("add back" your salary and benefits). That usually means the manager's cost didn't affect the purchase price at all, and sometimes it can even increase it. On the other hand, if a buyer anticipates an owner is doing the job of three people, they will reduce the EBITDA to cover the cost of the added management to adequately staff the company. This can lower the price of the company substantially.

Also, the amount of cash you receive up front (as opposed to notes, holdbacks and performance earn-outs) is inversely proportional to how important you are to day-to-day operations. And it is an understatement to say that cash at close is preferred.

With that in mind, let's talk about the second business owner. He typically worked 12 hours a day and often came in on weekends. He knew he needed to hire someone and he often complained to me about it. During a transaction, we do as much of the selling work as possible so the business owner can run the business. But selling a company takes time and effort from the owner as well, and this seller didn't have any time to spare. He was the only one who knew the market and had relevant sales data, but he didn't have time to write the information down and organize it. Potential buyers were frustrated by the lack of data about the company, and the seller was frustrated by the repetitive questions.

Worse, after buyers took a look, they saw a company that was completely reliant on the business owner. Would you want to pay a lot of cash to the business owner, and then hope he or she sticks around and, more importantly, stays excited and engaged? So, naturally, the offers had a lot of "back end" pay arrangements: performance earn-outs, partial buyouts and equity buy back provisions, seller notes, holdbacks, employment contracts, etc. One offer combined all of those. No one wants that.

The emotional roller coaster of selling your business

We once sold a business fairly quickly because a buyer "pre-empted' our marketing process by offering an amount that the seller was immediately comfortable with. In addition, it was a buyer that could obviously run and grow the company. So that part went very smoothly. Should be easy from here on out, correct?

However, it took six months to close. Financing was a challenge and there was a few issues that came up in due diligence. The buyer may have been almost perfect, but he was backed by a private equity group that was having trouble raising mezzanine financing (Financing that will take a little more risk than a bank, with higher rates and sometimes with equity). We though the financing was all but done, but just as we started serious due diligence the mezz lender backed out. We restructured the deal to make it a little more palatable for lenders. At the same time we contacted the backup offers we had to make sure they were notified that we may be approaching them very soon. Luckily we didn't have to rely on a backup offer. Another lender came through to solve that dilemma, only to have a payroll issue pop up in due diligence that threatened to change the EBITDA and thus the purchase price.

All of this on-again-off-again weighed heavily on the seller. I spent some long evenings talking to him, and I know my partner did as well. He had employees that were becoming suspicious and worried. His wife was worried about the future and he had to try to reassure her. He had family travel plans after the closing that were becoming at risk. Oh, and his way of life would change forever since the company that he built and identifies with will belong to someone else.

I remember selling my own company and it is a difficult period of time. There are so many "moving parts" of the transaction, so many things to worry about, that it becomes difficult to focus much on the deal, much less anything else.

Even as an M&A advisor, we can't help but get on that rollercoaster. You can't work that hard on a deal for seven months and not let it affect you. It affects my wife too: "Say, dear, are you ever going to get paid for that work you do?". But if I experienced the same emotional swings as a business owner I'm not sure I would be able to do this job in the long term - I'd have to take a month off after each closing to recover. We help the sellers and buyers through the process, and I truly believe it helps to have gone through it ourselves with our own businesses, but regardless I know there are some sleepless nights to be had.

For this example the deal did close, and he did get right on a plane with his family, if I remember to Hawaii.

Deal Extracts

Selling a business is not for the faint of heart. We had a client who was in a very hot field. When he first called us, he already had some unsolicited interest from an excellent strategic buyer that he wanted to sell to, so it looked like we should be able to execute a deal pretty quickly. This buyer proved to be a tough negotiator, dragging the offer process out over months until coming in with an offer that was well below what the seller would accept.

The next step was to get some competition for the buyer to drive up the valuation and help move the process along more quickly. We were successful on both counts. Negotiations proceeded more quickly and the pricing moved up. Eventually, the initial buyer won the day with an offer that was twice the original offer. With a letter of intent signed, we moved into the due diligence process.

Due diligence proceeded well at first, but issues came up during a site visit that almost killed the deal. That problem turned out to be more of a misunderstanding and we eventually worked our way past it.

After about three months it became clear that the seller was having a slow quarter due to some slowdowns on customers' projects using our client's product. The earnings from these programs were important to meeting the projections made by our client. Now we had to renegotiate the structure of the deal to avoid a major re-pricing. Our client took on more earn-out, thus sharing risk with the buyer.

Finally, we were in the home stretch and ready for the final meetings when the buyer's chief financial officer jumped in with a new issue. He questioned the manner in which revenue was recognized and sent the deal back into a tail spin.

Instead of closing on a Friday, we spent the weekend pulling together a variety of reports showing that the revenue recognition method was valid and closed on the following Tuesday.

Eight common mistakes business sellers make

You'll see a lot of "common selling mistakes" lists on M&A websites and many seem a little self-serving (for example, often they say the number one mistake is not using an intermediary). Rather than re-hash one of those lists, I put together my own set of selling no-nos.

1. **Not preparing the business financially**. Here is a short story that happened with a client. This owner had been aggressively using the company to pay for personal expenses and wanted to make adjustments in two dozen expense categories. He also admitted there was more that would remain unseen. A business is often only worth what the buyer can get financed, and you can't expect the lender to agree with excessive tax maneuvering. It is hard enough to convince a buyer. In this case, the seller had to take a lower price than they might have otherwise gotten. It would have been much better to start preparations two years before the sale. This seller, had he produced good clean books and paid a few more taxes, could have sold his business for more money and wouldn't have to live with the fear of an audit.

2. **Not preparing your business for a management hand-off**. The larger the business, the more thought needs to go into succession planning. While a sandwich shop may allow a buyer to step into full control within days of close, some businesses take a year or two. I heard the manager of a private equity group say, "I always ask myself, if the owner walks, does the business walk?" Ask yourself the same question. Then try to make and execute a plan that would make a new buyer comfortable. Similar to the financial planning, this can take a couple of years. The hand-off should be not only be clean organizationally and fiscally, it should be physically tidy as well. Start cleaning up the sites early (warehouses, offices, lab, etc.) just like you would do

when selling a house or a car.

3. **Delaying the process.** Delays kill deals. When in a transaction, keep it moving. Provide documents, fix equipment, answer questions, etc. Go in small steps if necessary.

4. **Surprises Kill Deals:** If something good or bad happens to the business we always counsel our clients; let us know and let's inform the buyer. NEVER let the buyer find out on their own, ALWAYS quickly notify the buyer of the event. The process of selling is a process of building trust between the buyer and the seller. If that trust is broken it may become impossible to recover from and the deal will die. Buyers want to only deal with people they feel they can trust. One of the most shocking surprises is when we found out one of the employees at a company was an ex-felon operating under an assumed name and was actually a pseudo-owner of the company.

5. **Unrealistic value expectations -** Many businesses for sale at any given time will not sell because the sellers have unrealistic expectations and will never get the offer they want. These sellers base their price on what they need or want, and not what the business is worth. Just about every seller can cite a reason why their business is worth more than a statistical analysis would indicate. I admit that sellers have convinced me on a number of occasions to turn down what I would consider fair offers for a higher price and I've yet to see that work. The best way to handle this problem is to not put a price on the company and allow the market to speak and negotiate the price up to the actual market price. However it is essential that be an understanding between the seller and the intermediary on an estimated market value. If the owner has unrealistic value expectations it would be a mistake to take the company to market. Both the buyer and the intermediary will be wasting a lot of time.

6. **Not reaching the right buyers, or trying to sell to just one buyer.** Many businesses are advertised on the web, and only the

web. It's a great resource. But medium or larger businesses and some unique small businesses need to be marketed in different ways. Private equity groups (professional investors) are in constant search of quality companies. Synergistic companies may wish to acquire for strategic reasons. If you think your company could use some custom marketing, ask for a marketing plan from your intermediary. If you get a blank look, you may want to go somewhere else. Our experience shows that the more buyers you have in the mix the greater the opportunity to drive up the price. Simply put, competition drives up price.

7. **Demanding all cash or being inflexible on terms.** The all-cash deal is the ultimate goal, however it is most likely that there will be some kind of structure to the deal. It's not uncommon to see some seller note in place or an earnout paid out over time based on future performance hurdles. During economic slowdowns, buyer nervousness will drive more frequent use of earn-out arrangements (future performance-based payouts). The way the buyer sees it, if the seller wants top dollar for his or her company because there is a bright future, but is unwilling to share in the risk, then there may a reason to suspect that rosy forecast. An inflexible seller will have a tough time closing a deal.

8. **Not using professionals appropriately.** I do recommend using an intermediary, and the appropriate one for your size. Get tax advice early, and realize it is possible that your current CPA isn't the best person to advise you, since they typically don't see a lot of M&A work. Pay for an attorney to review the agreements, but remember that his or her role is to advise, not control, the deal. As with your CPA, your current attorney may not be the best one to advise you on your transaction. Get one with deal experience. Experienced deal attorneys know which points to push and which to let go. They understand what is fair and reasonable in an M&A transaction.

Creating your dream team of professionals

All too often, a seller jumps into this process without much preparation. Before trying to sell, a transaction dream team of professionals should be brought together. Theoretically, this is who should be on the team:

- M & A advisor
- Transaction/deal attorney
- Financial/wealth advisor
- CPA

Let's take them one at a time.

M & A advisor

I have an entire chapter on this, so there's no need to discuss it here, except to identify those cases where you don't need one. You don't need an intermediary when selling to a family member, employee, or in cases where you are too small for even a business broker.

Otherwise, even if you have an unsolicited offer from a buyer, it helps to have an intermediary to create competition (or, at least, perceived competition) to make sure the price is fair (and market value), and to drive the process so the seller can run the business.

Having the right intermediary can make the difference of millions of dollars to a seller. An experienced intermediary knows when to push the buyer, when the buyer is being unreasonable and when they are just plain at the end of what they can offer. In addition, the intermediary can play the bad cop and leave you in the position to play the good cop. We can say the things that you may like to say but should not. We can get away with it where you cannot.

Transaction/Deal Attorney

Having an attorney with some empathy for the business owner is helpful. I've dealt with some seemingly cold, hard attorneys who fail to truly listen to the goals and desires of business owners. Some will "run off" with the deal to engage in an impressive battle with the other side's attorney, pushing the points they feel are important but disregarding the client's priorities. On the other hand, I've had excellent collaborative relationships with attorneys who took direction from the client.

It is important that your attorney has done more than one or two deals. Attorneys with too little deal experience have trouble understanding what is standard for business sales. It doesn't help the situation when an inexperienced attorney gets stuck on trivial issues, but fails to identify valid risks. Bringing in a new deal attorney can be difficult because many business owners have trusted attorneys who have become friends. In one case where we had that situation, we were able to successfully split the work, so the original attorney took direction from the deal attorney and did the work of organizing the contracts, exhibits, and agreements. Having the wrong attorney can be costly and even cost you the deal. We wish we did not have first-hand experience of this sort of thing, but unfortunately we have many cases of having the wrong attorney in place. Paying the attorney promptly every month can be a mistake, as they approach the end of the deal they recognize the gravy train is about to end. We have always found that a substantial payment upon completion of the deal keeps the attorney in the game.

Financial / Wealth Advisor

Get one – the sooner the better. Financial advisors (FA's) are somewhat like M & A advisors in that they will gladly spend time with you, even years before a liquidity event, hoping that they will be able to help you when the deal comes. They can also possibly set up some ways to divert or delay paying taxes when the money comes.

I know many business owners feel like meeting with an FA is like counting their chickens before they are hatched, but it is well worth the time to create an investment strategy that is ready when you are.

Remember that FAs are not all the same. Some are focused on growing wealth with more aggressive strategies. Others have wealth preservation as their main goal, and focus on diversification and lower-yielding, but safer, investments. It is a good idea to interview several and find one who makes you comfortable.

CPA

Obviously, your CPA will be involved with many aspects of the deal. Their first job will be producing financial statements that are current and ready for review by the deal team. They may work with your intermediary in getting a valuation and/or financial analysis done. Your CPA, however, often does not see enough business valuations to do a credible job of valuing a business. Many have a book or two on the shelf, but often that ends up creating a figure that doesn't represent the probable selling price Minimizing tax liability is often the biggest issue on the accounting side, so paying for a specialist is often a wise investment.

Good solid financial statements are needed to properly report the business to a buyer. Audit-level financial statement isn't required, but we typically like to see reviewed-level financial statements before proceeding without our process. Getting the financial information in order is often one of the longest delays preventing us from being a company to market in a timely manner. Get your financial reporting and statements in order and get "Reviewed" financial statements from your CPA for the last three years if you don't already have those.

Marketing the Business

Marketing = Competitive Bidding = Maximum Selling Price

Sales of businesses benefit from competition among buyers, as is the case with anything bought and sold. If a bidding situation develops, the selling price almost always goes higher or the terms improve. Given that, it is interesting to look at how businesses are typically marketed and sold.

Small Businesses (Sales less than $2-5 million)

Small businesses are typically sold by business brokers. To make a living, brokers typically handle seven to 10 listings at once and don't have the time to do much, if any, custom marketing. Their marketing efforts are usually limited to running ads on the business-for-sale websites.

These ads are relatively simple. Selling a small business is like selling a nice but standard automobile, like a 2010 Ford Explorer. You don't really need to describe much about the business because most people know what a Ford Explorer is, so, typically, you'll have a one-page summary. A deli, print shop or gas station is pretty easily understood, so you would want to describe the location, size, financial performance and include some photos.

These ads typically appear on sites like bizbuysell.com, bizquest.com, and businessesforsale.com. This method is effective since small business buyers know to search there. If you get multiple parties interested, it will be when the ads first appear. Marketing only on the websites makes sense for many small businesses, since these sites are geared to individual buyers who make up the majority of small business buyers.

Middle-Market Businesses (Sales $5 to $150 million)

If a small business is a Ford Explorer, a mid-sized company is more like a rare, antique automobile, like a 1948 Ferrari Barchetta. A buyer of a rare car is going to want to know a lot of detail about the body, electrical system, engine, maintenance history, and the like. Similarly, a middle market company needs a complete "book" that describes all aspects of the company, target market, competition, history, product line, reason for sale and other information.

The market for mid-sized businesses gets larger as the company gets bigger. Some individuals can still buy, but, more often, other companies and private equity groups will be your target market. They will most likely not be local but can come from virtually anywhere in the country, perhaps internationally too. The problem is that many companies are not actively looking to acquire a new business, though many will jump to buy when the right opportunity presents itself. Thus, the key to getting the most attractive bids for middle-market businesses is by marketing the company to a large number of individual buyers, potential corporate suitors and private equity groups, both domestically and internationally. The key is to not primarily use industry contacts or business-for-sale web listings, but to integrate good, old-fashioned marketing techniques like mailings and telephone calls, as well as the traditional print and web ads. Middle-market businesses are typically sold by M&A firms. To get the greatest number of bids, and attract the highest price, look for a firm that focuses on marketing.

Deal Extracts

In the middle market, marketing can make all the difference in getting a company sold for the best price. We had a new client, a medium-sized software as a service (SAAS) company in Moscow, Idaho. Moscow, I learned after visiting, is a very nice college town (the University of Idaho is located there) and residents enjoy a very nice quality of life. But it is not close to any major cities.

We marketed the company the way we normally do, with a combination of direct mail, follow up calls, email and direct calling to the top strategic and financial buyers. Many responded, but many dropped out after deciding that, logistically, it would be tough to have the company stay in Moscow. Strategic buyers wanted to move the company, but that really wasn't possible since they had built a very strong and talented team from the nearby university. Most of these people were not going anywhere. Several private equity buyers were interested, but, again, many dropped out when they realized that a board meeting could mean six flights total to get there and back.

However, we had 134 parties sign confidentiality agreements to receive a book and video about the company. Even with all of the fallout due to the remoteness of Moscow, we still had great interest with lots of potential buyers. We drove the process through our Q&A cycle and asked for initial offers, or indications of interest (IOIs, also known as first-round-bids). We received ten IOIs, which included price and structure.

The client reviewed the IOIs and picked three potential buyers they wanted to meet. After the meetings it was down to two. The client picked a buyer from the Silicon Valley for their expertise in technology, and the deal closed around 60 days later.

Large Businesses (Greater than $150 million in revenue)

Large companies are like a cargo ship. There are a limited number of qualified buyers that would be interested, so you would hire a specialized broker who knows the industry and can approach the buyers he has in his database. A large marketing campaign is not needed. For large businesses, typically an investment banker is hired who has industry specific knowledge that can be used to find buyers and structure an appropriate deal.

If the owners of Yahoo! wanted to sell, there are a limited number of companies that would be interested, and a good investment bank working in that industry would probably know all of them. The goal, of course, is still to get multiple bids.

The Competitive Bidding Process

I've tried to make this book generic and informative and not specific information about Woodbridge, but the best illustration of a competitive bidding process is to examine the process we use at Woodbridge International. It shows the international flavor of the marketing and how we use timing and the flow of information to enhance the competitive nature of the process.

75% of the time, we sell companies to a buyer our client had never heard of.

That is an amazing statistic when you think about it, and shows the power of marketing to a wide audience in order to generate competition. It is somewhat of an overused phrase, but it is true that "you can't get market price unless you go to the market".

Market Far and Wide
For a middle market company we have found that you really can't know (e.g. pull out of your rolodex) who is available and ready to buy at a specific time. So we'll build up a business plan of who to go to and what countries to target and we will typically end up with a fairly large list. Typical numbers are 2,500 private equity groups and 2,500 strategic buyers.

We have a research group that gathers strategic names from business intelligence databases, industry and trade journals, web searches and of course asking our clients. Of course there are always some "black list" names that our client doesn't want us to talk to. In fact, one challenge for us is what to say to these black listers when they call. Although honest, "Sorry, but our client really doesn't like you" doesn't seem like the best answer. We usually try to come up with something that is also true, but not quite so specific.

The following pyramid diagram is data from a deal that started in January and closed in September of the same year. Although we also have an office in Brazil, in this case it was decided to market to North America, Europe and Asia. In this case an Asian buyer won the day and walked away with the company (a company involved with lighting).

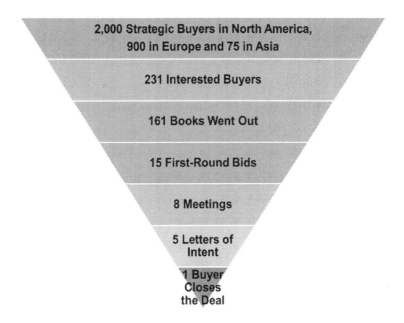

By the way, the marketing is done in a blind manner so buyers don't know the identity of the company until they sign a confidentiality agreement. In the example above, 161 parties knew the identity of the company. Granted, sometimes it is a challenge to craft good marketing materials that don't give away the identity, but we always work with the client to come up with something compelling, but not specific.

The timeline for this example is as follows:

Date	Process	Activity
October 2010	Prep Company Materials	Financials, Book, Video
December 2010	Marketing Research	Research market, create marketing plan, build lists
January 2011	Launch	Direct mail, email, calls, web ads, print ads in select countries
March 2011	First round bids	Buyer qualification, Q&A
April 2011	Management meetings	Analyze and select buyers to meet with
May 2011	LOI Signed	Negotiations with final buyers
June 2011	Due Diligence	Financial, legal and operational due diligence, plus financing.
September 2011	Deal Closed	

The following are some important points when dealing with a large group of buyers, some financial buyers like private equity and some strategic.

1. **Fully prepare marketing materials and financials of the company before the marketing "launch".** Besides the book and a financial analysis, we even produce a short video with a professional videographer so a large number of prospective buyers can see and hear from the owners as well as take a short tour of the business. The important point is that all materials should be completely ready to go, as typically some buyers will ask for the information immediately, within an hour or two of the marketing launch.

2. **Control the process.** A competitive process requires an actual

structured process – you can't let the buyers dictate what the next steps are. It takes some discipline because some good, strong buyers will have their own idea on what to do next and it is easy to get excited and potentially lose control of the process.

In fact, I've often had a buyer that tries to preempt the process by trying to set up a meeting with the owners right away or even negotiate a final price. In fact, as I write this I took a call from a buyer who wanted to know what the bottom line price I had agreed to with a seller before taking the selling engagement. Really, he just came out and asked. I was polite and said yes, we often have a ballpark bottom line selling price that we agree to with a client, but it is kind of a like an attorney-client relationship and isn't something I can share. I told him if and when he put in his first round bid I could give him a sense of where he was at and tried to be cheerful as I said it. He grumbled but said OK. Having said this, we have pre-empted the process for a good buyer that offers an excellent price that the seller agrees to. If it makes everyone happy, why not? But it is rare because usually the main thing that makes our client happy is the best price, and that typically only comes with competition.

3. **Timing is Critical.** We at Woodbridge have a tested process that we know works in terms of the timing of the different marketing channels we use. But really it is just common sense and careful thought.

   For example, if you email your strongest buyer prospects right away, they will likely respond right away. In addition, they will not need much time to digest the opportunity because they probably already know the industry and maybe familiar with the company. However, if you want to get other buyers involved you'll need to stall those strongest buyers you contacted while others come up to speed. It is rarely a good idea to stall a buyer.

   If you look at the speed of the marketing channel (email vs. direct mail vs. calling vs. print advertising vs. web advertising) and who the target is, then you can proceed accordingly.

4. **Maintain Momentum**. Good timing often means slowing things down just a little so all buyers can reach the finish line (bids) at the same time. Good momentum means keeping things moving and taking advantage of the enthusiasm of the buyers.

   Sometimes, unfortunately, some buyers get left behind. A few large corporations can barely have their legal department turn around a confidentiality agreement in the time it takes for us to go through the entire bidding process. It is frustrating, but I try to be pleasant and I'll rarely shut them down completely, and I'll often try to get them back up to speed later in the process. But some just drop out. I'd much rather keep the process going and take advantage of the momentum then to stop and wait for one buyer.

5. **Publish Dates.** We publish dates for our selling process. The first date after launch is the date that questions are due. The second date is for the publication of the Q&A document and a financial update, and the third date is the date that first round bids are due. The Q&A process, in which we publish all questions and answers to all buyers, is powerful in that it helps create a true market with better informed buyers, and it has the secondary benefit of making sure that all buyers know that there is competition (for they may receive 100 Q&As after having submitted 5 questions).

6. **Keep a focus on business performance**. It is worth repeating that a common deal-killer is a lack of performance during negotiations, so our process is also structured so the owners can keep a focus on their business. We typically have so many prospective buyers that having management conference calls with each one could stall the company. Plus, they get kind of monotonous because each buyer will start off asking the same questions (Why are you selling, how long will you stay for a transition, etc.). This is another reason our process includes a written Q&A document that allows the owner to answer common questions once.

   Of course, it is human nature to be distracted with the selling process anyway. How many companies have responded? What do they think of my company? However, is absolutely critical to stay focused enough to essentially hit the performance numbers that were communicated to the buyers. The deal depends on it.

7. **Let the market dictate price.** The free market will tell you what the price is. We've had sellers that would have asked for much less than they got – a difference of millions of dollars. Although to be fair we also have companies that don't sell for what the owners had hoped to get. However, with an exhaustive effort to market the company to a broad market, at least we all know it was a price determined by a market of multiple buyers.

8. **Control the meetings**. Instead of having a buyer meeting occasionally throughout the process, which can be quite disrupting, we go through a "first round bid" process where each interested buyer must submit a non-binding Indication of Interest that includes price (or at least a price range) and an indication of deal structure. We then present an analysis of the first round bids to the client and together we decide who to meet with. Therefore the client meets only with qualify buyers that have already indicated what they would pay. In addition, the meetings all happen within a relatively short amount of time, sometimes in sequential days if we can schedule that.

    A common mistake is to accept invitations to buyer meetings as they come up early in the process. The business owner will end up spending significant time and energy with buyers that end up offering low bid prices.

9. **Have Options**. I like to think of my job as providing options to my clients. Often a client will say that they don't think private equity makes sense and why waste the time? However there may be some private equity firms that own a company that is very strategic and may want to buy. From my experience, you absolutely don't know where the ultimate buyer may come from. In addition, each buyer will have a different price and how to structure the deal. Thus we try to get an agreement to do a full, 100%-effort marketing job with each

engagement, bringing buyers along and presenting as many options as we can to our client. Plus it helps the competitive process to have multiple engaged buyers. Below is a very condensed version of the analysis presented to the client in the example above with the various options. These are real numbers from five firm offers (LOIs, or Letters of Intent). By the way, these numbers represent about 6x to 6.5x of EBITDA in this particular case.

Prospective Buyer	Stock or Asset Deal	Value	Cash At Closing	Seller Note	Earn-out
1	Stock with Section 338(h)(10) election	$14m	$11m	No	Yes (until end of current year)
2	Asset	$10.5m	$8.5m	Yes - 6% interest	No
3	Stock	$11.4	$7.5m	No	Yes (over the next few years)
4	Stock	$14m	$7.0m	$3m at 5% over 5yrs.	Yes (over the next few years)
5	Asset or Stock	$10m	$10m	Possible	No

10. **A signed LOI is not time to celebrate.** After an LOI is signed, it is due diligence time, and sometimes things go wrong for various reasons. A competitive environment with multiple buyers is great because most of the time the losing bidders will stay in backup positions on buying the company. That provides a lot of peace of mind during the due diligence.

Deal Extracts

I would like to think that my amazing negotiating skills and ample powers of persuasion will result in millions, or even tens of millions, more dollars in my client's pockets. But it isn't so. The buyers pay more not because of me (although I like to think I help), but because of competition. Competition means there is the fear of loss and the validation of value that comes with having other parties bidding higher prices.

My client told me that Buyer A was the prize – they were a global billion dollar company that he would be proud to have sold his company to. Unfortunately, Buyer A was extremely confident in the value they placed on my client's company, and told me the price would not change much from where they started. When the first round bids came in, here is where we were at.

Buyer	Value	Cash	Earnout
A (Strategic)	$35 million	$15 million	$20 million
B (Strategic)	$45 million	$25 million	$20 million
C (Private Equity)	$36 million	$20 million	$16 million
D (Private Equity)	$60 million	$40 million	$20 million
E (Private Equity)	$60 million	$40 million	$20 million

The buyer with the best strategic fit was offering the lowest price and the lowest cash-at-close by a wide margin. I could have tried saying something like: "My clients would really like $23 million more in cash on the top of the $15 million that you said was the upper limit. If you do that we have a deal." I'm not sure that would have worked.

However my clients did end up with $23 million more in cash ($38 million total cash-at-close), and they got it from Buyer A. Why? All I had to do is point out that we had two offers for $60 million and although my client would love to be bought by Buyer A, they just couldn't walk away from that much money (not many people would!).

Although $38 million cash was still a little shy of the cash components of the other offers, the total package with the ability to hit the earnout targets was valued more highly by my clients.

Negotiations

Timing is also important when planning when to negotiate with buyers. You don't want to lose the individual momentum of any one specific buyer by starting to early and needing to slow it down because you need to allow enough time for other buyers to come up to speed and ask questions.

In fact, we will (generally) not start real negotiations until after the buyer has put in their first round bid and then had a chance to visit and meet with the owners and management. We may point out when they are so low in their first round bid that they will likely not make the final round, but if they are in that top group of bids that will be invited for meetings, we'll leave it at that. Besides, it is not even very realistic to start asking for price concessions before the buyer has seen the company.

We'll hope for quality management meetings (buyer/seller meetings) which back up the book, video and all the conversations that we've had to date. For the sake of timing we'll try to push all the meetings into a fairly short time period (although we'll make sure to make them all long enough to give each buyer time to get their questions answered). It works out pretty well that way anyway because it is generally easier on our client to do them all at once then to spread them out over months.

THEN the real negotiations start. The buyers have had ample chance to get questions answered before first round bids, have met with our clients to hear the story and see the company, and hopefully are now excited about landing the deal. Now is the time to use the competitive nature of the process to guide the buyers to not only maximize the purchase price but also a structure that our clients are looking for.

International Marketing

We all know that it's a smaller and smaller world with a smorgasbord of international companies doing business in every country.

As an example, I went to Brazil recently to work on a deal representing a company in Sao Paulo. My clients were excited because Brazil is a high growth market, and their company would be highly sought after by US and other international companies. At the same time I was down there, an old friend from Brazil was in California looking for high tech investments to invest in. So I was down there involved with US investment money flowing south to Brazil, while at the same time he was in the US dealing with Brazilian investment money flowing north.

I did sell that Brazilian company to a US company (that was owned by a British company) and was also involved in selling a US company to a Chinese buyer. In fact Woodbridge has done more international deals over the past 5 years than ever before and we have even changed our name from Woodbridge Group to Woodbridge International. For example, the deal illustrated in the last chapter on competitive process was a US company sold to a Asian company.

Basically, we take each deal on its own merit and decide whether to go international with it. For example, at the time of this writing we are just launching a chemical distribution company and decided that it made sense (beside the US) to market it to Europe and South America, but not to Asia (where the chemicals come from).

Each country has its own marketing techniques and quirks, so the Woodbridge US team works closely with the Woodbridge team in each foreign region to do most effectively contact potential buyers. For example, we use a call center to call behind all the first class mailings that go out to the strategic buyers in the US (the M&A advisor personally calls the "hot list", but we can't call a few thousand). In Europe that technique doesn't work so the office there relies on first class mail, email and direct calling when appropriate. Thank goodness for the internet, as we rely on a cloud based database system to track the marketing activity globally.

Deal Extracts

Culture can make or break a deal.

I flew down to Brazil to help with due diligence on a company I had sold there. I realized on the way down that nothing had been done on DD so I was anxious to get to work. My long flight got in at 8 am and with traffic in Sao Paulo I didn't arrive at the office until 11:00. As soon as I arrived my clients said, "hey, it's about lunch time, let's go for a meal". I knew what that meant, a nice leisurely meal with that amazing Brazilian coffee afterwards. I really wanted to just dive into work, but luckily I knew what I should do – relax and go have a meal and not be a pushy American. We had lunch and we talked family and we talked airplanes and we talked about everything but work. The coffee was fantastic and the lunch lasted hours. In the end, what it did was helped my relationship with my client and really didn't impact the work much.

A week later the buyer came down for meetings and did not want to go out to lunch. Instead they wanted sandwiches brought in for a working lunch. My clients laughed and made fun of the American "working lunch", which made me realize how lucky I was to have gone to lunch that first day and not tried to just jump into the work.

On the day before the closing on that same deal, a stalemate occurred between buyer and seller. The seller expected some give and take, as often (apparently always) happens in Latin America. The American buyer was taking a firm stand ("the deal is the deal, and I can't do anything else. Sorry."). I talked with the American buyer about what I perceived as a clash of cultures. He needed to give something up. Anything. There is always something that can be done, and it doesn't have to be something that affects the purchase price. With some creativity negotiations continued, some concessions were made, and the deal was closed.

Earnings: EBITDA

The term "earnings before interest, taxes, depreciation, and amortization" (EBITDA) is typically used for middle market companies, companies usually earning more than $500,000. The term is generally used to show an investor/buyer (vs. an owner/operator) how much a company is earning. The investor does not actively run the company, and must pay a professional manager to do that for him. Thus, the manager's salary is expensed and is included in the earnings calculation. (It is not added back into earnings like with smaller companies). Simply put, EBITDA is a way for an investor to measure the return on investment he will receive should he purchase a company.

I should mention that advanced investors go further than EBITDA and use discounted free cash flow or discounted cash flow (DCF) analysis. EBITDA is not a true cash flow, and really what an investor wants to know is how much cash a business will generate in the future. A DCF model includes taxes, working capital, growth, and anything else that impacts cash flow. It then discounts those future cash flows to a present value. DCF is pretty hard to do correctly because it can be very difficult to estimate future cash flows and to calculate a discount rate factor for risk, so it isn't used all that often.

Sometimes small businesses (typically those sold using SDE as the valuation metric) are sold with nothing left in the business – no cash, no payables, and no accounts receivables. The new owner needs to recognize that and leave themselves enough cash to fund the working capital needs of the business.

It is important to understand that middle market companies (typically those that use EBITDA as the valuation metric), are sold with "gas in the car". That is, a new owner buys the company with the expectation that enough working capital (including AR, AP, inventory, etc.) is left in the company to continue to run it. To express this another way, the buyer has a right to all assets that are being used to produce the level of EBITDA as presented.

That doesn't mean that all cash is always left in the business. Excess cash, which would be the amount of extra cash on hand that isn't required to run the business, is taken out and "taken home" with the seller.

EBITDA attempts to standardize the earnings number by excluding items that are variable and discretionary from company to company. For example, one company may have a heavy debt load while another may have none. So we exclude interest expense from EBITDA. A buyer then calculates what his specific debt load will be and can adjust the earnings number to fit his situation. Same with taxes – some companies have different tax strategies, so EBITDA uses a pretax earnings number. Depreciation and amortization are non-cash expenses, and also are more of an accounting method rather than real-world depreciation of assets, so we exclude that as well.

However, don't completely discount depreciation of assets. A smart seller will capitalize and depreciate assets (instead of expensing them) in the years before a sale to boost earnings. A smart buyer will remove depreciation, but then look at expected capital expenditures ("CapEx") so they know they will have the cash flow in the future to buy needed assets and continue to improve the business.

Deal Extracts

Sometimes sellers forget that earnings are the underpinnings of their company's value. I remember one situation where we had a deal in due diligence with a letter of intent and an agreement on price. The acquiring company sent in a team to look at the books. They spent a few days there and when they got back home, they called us and said they were "shocked" by what they found. The earnings number projected for the year was far below those presented to them previously.   *Uh-oh.*

It turns out the audit team had used internal planning documents that were completely unadjusted.. The owner had his personal airplane expenses included and some legal expenses that would not continue after a sale. In addition, the owner was an engineer, and in his mind (I'm an engineer too, so I can say this) he didn't count future sales for the year unless he had a firm, signed contract. If you asked him if he expected additional sales he would say, "Of course, but these with the signed contracts are the ones we absolutely know we have." In other words, his internal sales projections looked terrible because they only included 100% contracted sales.

So the expenses were too heavy and the revenue was too light. Once we pointed this out to the buyers they understood this, and a crisis was averted.

Adjusting earnings – Add-backs

The value of a business is almost always dependent on earnings. But it is **adjusted** earnings, called Adjusted EBITDA, that is used for the valuation. For instance, EBITDA is often adjusted to make sure it is before taxes, interest and depreciation. "Owner's benefit" can also be an adjustment, and that can be a tricky add-back.

Remember, EBITDA reflects the earnings flowing to an investor that owns a company. We will often work with an owner-operator that doesn't necessarily pay himself market rate – he pays himself what he wants to, or what he can. It may be far more than market rate, or often it is far less (for example, the owner takes out earnings via dividends or simply leaves it in the business to fund growth). A fair and accurate EBITDA number includes the market rate wages and benefits of a manager that doesn't own the company.

Often the easiest way to do this is to add back ALL the current owner's wages and benefits. Then you subtract out the market rate wages and benefit of a professional manager. Of course, it often isn't that simple. We'll see multiple owners of one company (such as a husband/wife team) and they don't work full time, yet they do completely different functions. How many people would the new owner have to hire? Two half-time workers? Sometimes we see a spouse working full-time in the company and not getting paid at all. In that case, we have to do a negative adjustment to account for the fact that a new buyer is unlikely to find someone to work for free.

Other add-backs for owner's benefit are health insurance, life insurance, pension and any owner perks, such as personal expenses written off as company expenses. We have even seen companies with 7 digit "charitable contributions" where their chosen charity project was a new house for themselves. The purpose is to try to determine what benefits a new owner would enjoy and what discretionary expenses a new owner may decide to spend according to his own taste.

Sometimes it gets awkward when the owner is taking so many perks that it really amounts to tax fraud. Everyone does some tweaking, such as putting the families' cell phones into the company, or writing off car expenses when the company doesn't really use the car. These are generally accepted as "legitimate" add-backs – even by the SBA, which is after all a part of the government. You can usually add back a few tougher items, like a son or daughter who is on the payroll but isn't actually working. But at some point you have to draw the line (or the buyer will draw one for you).

Other add-backs are one-time items such as moving expenses, some legal expenses or major repairs. Once you have the correct add-backs folded back into earnings, you then have your adjusted EBITDA, and this number can be used to compare the company to similar companies or even across industries for the purposes of valuation or showing a new buyer what he or she can make from the business.

Some M & A firms (and sellers) get very aggressive when it comes to adjusting financial statements. Beside automatic add-backs for taxes, depreciation and interest (these of course are added back by definition), you can also make adjustments for the aforementioned one-time expenses and discretionary expenses. But it isn't a cut and dried formula and it takes a little common sense to apply the rules. The basic premise of these adjustments is that you are trying to estimate what a buyer will experience in the future as the new owner. It is that simple.

If as an owner you are doing the work of two people the add-backs need to be adjusted to accommodate for potentially adding another employee. I have seen buyers trying to find ways to increase expenses and reduce the recast EBITDA. It is our job to make sure that in the initial presentation of the financials we have properly accounted for the proper expenses on a go forward basis and not have any surprises from a buyer poking holes in the presentation.

I was reviewing a financial statement on behalf of a client who was looking to buy a multiple-location, high-end closet and garage-organizing business. Almost every account had an adjustment and I was having a hard time taking it all in. Why, for example, was there an adjustment of $16,500 for tools and equipment? I was told it was a one-time expense, and the tools purchased last a long time. OK, then why the adjustment the year prior? Different tools I was told. Wasn't it probable that each year there are tools to purchase? In other words, the M & A Advisor was saying that the new owner would not have to purchase any tools or equipment to sustain the business. That was probably not the case.

How about travel, in which almost everything was added back? Well, I was told, much of that was personal, and the remainder was to go to an industry convention that they go to each year. But, in a buyer/seller meeting, the seller told the buyer the convention was great and taught them a great deal about running the business. Therefore, going to the trade show is important to running the business and therefore not an expense that can be legitimately added back.

The financials were also packed with personal expenses, like airplane fares, phone bills, and undisclosed credit card purchases. You learn quickly in this business that adjustments for personal expenses that were run through the company for tax reasons are quite common. You often hear that "everyone does it" and practically everyone does. But there is a limit. The IRS has a limit, the lenders have a different limit, and the individual buyers also have a limit. At some point, the buyers start to wonder, "If the seller goes to great lengths to hide that much money from the IRS, might they also try to take a little extra money from me?"

That was exactly what I was thinking in the case of the closet company. I asked to see the details of the personal credit card purchases. I was told no, and given the explanation that the card the owner's wife's personal credit card and that that should be enough evidence that the purchases were purely personal (but paid for by the company).

You know that a company's value is directly affected by earnings, more specifically, future earnings. It became apparent to me that a new owner would not enjoy the profits that the seller and advisor had calculated, and thus the business wasn't worth the asking price. We rejected some of the add-backs and came up with an offer based on the same multiple of earnings that the asking price used. The seller became quite angry – so angry, in fact, that we never heard from him again.

The seller did not sell the business that year. He is working with his third advisor, and as of this writing, the business is on the market again at a much lower price – well below our offer. Not that I was keeping track. Selling a business is about building trust between the buyer and the seller. If that trust is broken sometimes it is impossible to restore and the deal crumbles.

The Essence of Business Valuation

Deal Extracts

One thing I like about this job is visiting companies and seeing their operations and experiencing first-hand how they make money, and how they add value to our economy. This trip took me up the coast of California to a notoriously foggy but beautiful town. It was a nice little manufacturing company but they had a unique situation.

Future earnings equal value and typically you can classify a company as stable and low risk or high growth yet risky. In fact, this is what basically separates private equity (stable and low risk) with venture capital (high growth yet risky). This company had one of the most stable businesses I've seen. Rock solid with a great and diverse customer base and EBITDA just under $2 million. Yet they had been pursuing a high growth opportunity and had already spent almost $2 million on the research and development to make that opportunity happen.

The challenge was placing a value on the entire company. The core business was so stable (meaning a buyer could be comfortable those earnings would continue in the future) we could probably get 100% cash up front for the business, except it wasn't high growth so the multiple wouldn't be that high – probably between four and five. However, what about this new business they were poised to get and had spent time and money on – yet didn't have a dollar of revenue from? How do you value that?

We don't price a company — we let the market speak via competition. Often we don't even provide much guidance if the facts speak for themselves. However in this case I spent a lot of time with buyers discussing the two segments of the business and how their offers could include cash, notes and earnouts that would compensate the sellers for the stable core business and the potential upside on the new business.

Future earnings equal value

What is the fundamental value of a business? There are a lot of "rules of thumb" out there for business valuations. Multiples of earnings, multiples of revenue, discounted cash flow, book value, and so on.

It is easy to get caught up in all of this and lose sight of the reason you are going to all this trouble. You can often answer complex valuation questions by remembering the bigger picture and applying some common sense.

Valuation comes down to how much money the business will produce in the future and the risk factors associated with generating that money. For larger companies, great effort is placed in modeling the future, then discounting that stream of cash to present-day dollars. Two valuation approaches based on this premise are the income approach and the discounted free cash flow approach. This can be incredibly complex, right down to calculating the discount rate to be used.

Small and mid-size companies also use future earnings. However, since it is too difficult and risky to predict the future, we assume the past will indicate what the future will bring. Thus, when a mergers and acquisitions firm or a business appraiser says you are worth five times your earnings, there is a big assumption that those earnings will continue into the future. Everything is based on that basic assumption.

Here are a couple real-world examples of how earnings impact valuations, based on my own experience. I once had a multimillion-dollar deal fall completely apart during due diligence (I was representing the buyer) because we found out at close of escrow that the seller was not going to pay off the long-term operating lease on a $300,000 computer-controlled milling machine. The problem was that the lease payments had been added back to the earnings used to price the business.

I didn't think it was a major issue, and I calmly laid out ways around this problem. The seller could pay off the lease, or we could include the lease payments in the earnings number and recalculate the business price, or we could take the future lease payments and discount them to present-day dollars and use that for a price adjustment. I said that we wouldn't pay for earnings that don't continue into the future. You see, the price of the business, in this case, was based on four times the historical earnings, but those historical earnings wouldn't continue into the future unless there was no lease payment. We were talking about a $250,000 difference in value for the business. The seller was furious and pointed to a document that said that lease payments should be added back to earnings calculations. However, those calculations were based on the assumption of a payoff of the lease. Unfortunately, that was the end of that deal.

It is customary for a seller to pay off long term debt and/or equipment leases at the closing. There are exceptions of course, for example if you bought brand new equipment that isn't being used to produce earnings. In this case it makes sense that the buyer pays for the equipment as an investment, just as the seller did (assuming the seller can convince the buyer the equipment will bring in new revenue and earnings).

Another example was a client with a combination brick-and-mortar/web business that had a great URL / web site. After we supplied an estimate of the business value, he wanted to know why we forgot to value the web address, as it must be worth quite a bit. However, he had that address for years, and thus its earnings-producing potential was already built into past earnings of the business, and the basis for predicting future earnings. In other words, there was no additional value. He then said "Oh well, then I'll let them have the website software, but I'll just keep the web address." I then had to explain why he couldn't keep the web address and still charge full value for the business. Those all-important historical earnings include the use of that web address, and without it, a new buyer could not produce those earnings. In fact, without it, you are not even sure how much revenue and earnings will drop, and the valuation becomes much more complicated.

Why use Multiples of Earnings

It is common to hear M & A advisors say "That business is worth four or five times earnings." But what does that mean? We know that value is really based on future earnings. If you take a future earnings stream and discount that back to current dollars, that is vaguely similar to just taking past earnings and multiplying that by a factor (assuming that past earnings predict future earnings).

Multiples of EBITDA

Medium-size companies (above $1,000,000 in earnings) typically use a multiple of EBITDA for valuations, and they typically range from three to seven, with four to six being common

The valuation multiples of companies grow with size. For example, the multiple for a company with $1,000,000 in earnings will trend towards five, while companies over $10 million in earnings will trend towards 8 (other things being equal). In fact, you can pretty much trend the multiples right up into the large public company arena. The P/E ratio of a public company is roughly the same as an EBITDA multiple, although the main difference is P/E is based on after tax earnings so the multiple will naturally be higher. A quality public company's P/E ratio is typically between 10 and 20.

Larger companies with EBITDA more than $20 or $30 million can often be valued by comparing with similar public companies. Smaller ones generally have too many additional risk factors to be able to estimate value using this method.

Middle Market Business Valuation

Valuation guide and chart

The following is a diagram summing up my variation on the EBITDA multiple valuation metric for middle market businesses (businesses with earnings between around $1 million and $20 million). The basic rule of thumb valuation for a growing company with about a million in earnings is a value of five times EBITDA. Why five? Simply because the average selling price for many businesses turns out to be five times EBITDA (As I mentioned, higher for companies with significantly more than a million in earnings). Do middle market buyers really just use a multiple of five when buying a business? No, they will perform extensive analysis and run financial models for every deal. However, after all the analysis and models are created and run, some deals end up below five, some above, and the average has remained around five. This also assumes modest growth.

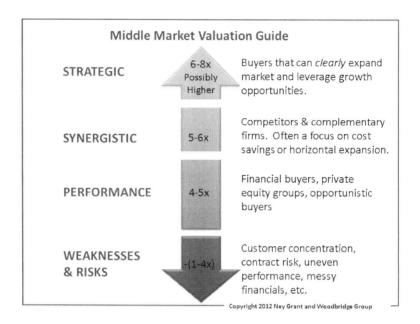

This brings us to the valuation guide. What the chart says is that the five times base value assumes the company has a stable history of performance and no significant blemishes. A stable financial performance is the most basic component and the foundation of a valuation.

EBITDA can be enhanced by a buyer who can reduce costs and take advantage of other synergies, and because of that, the synergistic buyer can afford to pay a little more for the company. They will not want to, of course, but with a competitive situation and negotiation, the price can be driven up.

A strategic buyer who can go further, take the company to a new level of sales growth and open up new opportunities (usually as well as the cost synergies above) can afford to pay even more. Note that it still comes down to financial performance and earnings, but the strategic buyer is betting they can pay now for later earnings. Unfortunately, the true strategic buyer who will pay a substantial premium is somewhat rare.

Interestingly, every buyer will come up with their own price and structuring of a deal. For as many years as I have been doing this I have never seen two offers that came in on a business that were the same. It is not uncommon to see a valuation range with as much as a 50% difference in value from the highest offer to the lowest offer. This is why it is so important to get multiple offers and understand how *the market* is valuing the company. We say if you have one offer you have no solid offers. Because, how do you know if that one offer is a good one or a bad one?

I've yet to run across the perfect company. There are always blemishes, and if they are serious enough to cause a risk that future earnings may not actually turn out as expected, these blemishes work to pull down the valuation. Do you have one customer (or supplier) who contributes more than 25 percent of your revenue? Messy financials? Lots of adjustments to the earnings? These can pull that five times multiple down to a four or lessen the cash at closing and increase a seller note or earnout. Or if you have a strategic buyer, perhaps they'll only pay five times instead of six.

A professional valuation uses a similar process to this guide by taking a close look at your fundamental performance and/or looking at whether your particular market has a history of strategic buyers, and then they discount the value based on the some of the risk factors they find. If you can stand back and take an objective look at your business, you should be able to estimate a multiple for your business.

Value premium for "quality" businesses

Let's say we have two companies – A, Inc. and B Co. – that each have $2 million in earnings for the past five years and are in similar industries. What could make A worth more than B? The answer will surprise many business owners.

Some may argue that if they both make the same in earnings and those earnings are stable, then, theoretically, they should be valued the same. However, quality does matter and quality companies can demand a premium. But what does "quality" mean in terms of an increased purchase price?

Some attributes that don't define "quality"

Each year I get two or three business owners who believe they have such a great web presence, including a URL coveted in their industry, that they should get a premium for their company. Let's say B Co. has the URL "widget.com" for the widget industry. That is nice, but the fact is that B is earning $2 million annually partly because they already have that URL. That cool name is already built into earnings, and thus built into the sales price. The only bonus a buyer gets is that, if B Co. ever shuts down, you could sell the name "widget.com" to a competitor. In other words, having a great website doesn't mean quality in terms of purchase price. A great location, most patents, a talented workforce, and other positives about your business are already built into earnings and purchase price as well. It all boils down to: "what are the assets earning in profits?". They will pay you for what you have done but they will buy you because of their belief in the future potential of the business.

I also get owners who are proud of keeping their company debt free and believe someone should pay more for such a company. These owners should be proud and I'm always impressed when I witness what they have accomplished. But the fact is that, as a company grows, it will attract professional investors as buyers, and these investor/buyers will use some debt to grow the company – that is how you can use other people's money to leverage your return on investment. These buyers will also be impressed, but they will not care too much about keeping it debt free and will not pay a premium for that. That being said we like to see a debt free company because as a seller you will get to keep all the proceeds of the sale and not see the cash at closing reduced by paying off debt.

Attributes that define "quality"

A "quality" company is one that makes buyers comfortable. A "quality" company is one with low risk. What kinds of things am I talking about?

Clean financials: There is nothing more comforting to a buyer than knowing that $2 million in earnings really is $2 million in earnings. If the owner has been cheating heavily on taxes, the buyer's comfort level goes down. If the financials are messy and fuzzy, the comfort level goes down. Buyers also like to see consistency in the financials and stability with a long standing relationship with a noted accounting firm.

Management: Buyers focus on the continuity of the business, and management plays a key role in that. Is the business dependent on the owner? Is the owner staying? Is there a management team in place if the owner is leaving? If all the pieces are not in place, buyers start to feel uncomfortable. Buyers will pay a premium for a business in which the owner has built a solid management team and the business is not heavily dependent upon the owner/founder/entrepreneur.

Customers: Are the customers committed to buying in the future? Is any single customer responsible for more than 15 percent of revenue? Are they good at paying in a timely manner? Could a new owner expand the relationship with the current customer base? Strategic buyers are frequently motivated to acquire in order to obtain a new customer base.

The future: A smart buyer takes a look at the $2 million historical earnings over 5 years, but focuses on the future. They take a close look at booked orders, market trends, life stages of the company's products and services, etc. Anything that can make the buyer feel comfortable that the $2 million in earnings is sustainable and can grow will move that company into the quality territory. The opportunity for the future and the buyer's ability to tap into that potential will be directly reflected in the price they pay. That is why it is so important to identify the value drivers of the business and spend a lot of time talking about future growth potential.

All of the above: Although I said a web address or a talented team doesn't matter, they do when taken together. A quality company has several characteristics that, when considered alone, wouldn't bump up a price. But together, these characteristics cause a buyer to say, "There isn't a lot to worry about with this company – I could imagine owning this."

The purchase price of business still comes down to future earnings, but with a quality company those earnings have less risk associated with them and less risk commands a premium.

Note that we're talking about a quality company – not a perfect company, which doesn't exist. So if you are disappointed while reading this because you see problems and challenges in your business, don't despair. There are problems and challenges with every business, even a quality one.

Deal Extracts

Valuing companies is more of art than a science, and sometimes it gets a little confusing. We had a client who flipped homes, in a major way. His company was producing around $7 million in earnings, but he also had investment funds set up that he used as capital to buy the homes. He paid his investors a very healthy return on investment of about 40 percent per year.

At first, we tried to collapse the entire business model into something we were more familiar with, assuming one buyer bought the company and put up the money to fund the home purchases. This jacks up the EBITDA substantially – along with the value – but it also requires a hefty capital investment of around $50 million dollars onto the balance sheet as working capital. However, the principal amount of the working capital is not at risk like in other companies and it can be returned to the buyer at any time. It really is a different model and requires free cash flow analysis and ROI analysis to get a handle on it.

You could also take the simpler view that his earnings are $7 million, and that the returns provided to the investors are the cost of capital required to be able to use large sums of money that is required to execute his business model. Furthermore, you could say that the buyer of the company and the investor could be the same person. That is, a buyer could buy the company, kick out all the existing investors and then use his own money to fund the company and thus capture the 40 percent ROI himself.

In the end, we did a combination of the two scenarios. The value, of course, is really the value perceived by the buyer. In this case, we presented the value both ways and it became obvious how this particular buyer perceived it. This buyer had a large amount of money he wanted to put to work and the notion of setting up an investment fund appealed to him. We had to convince him that paying a premium for this company was the price he had to pay to be able to do this.

Return on investment

There is a staggering difference between the return on investment that a venture capitalist seeks (often more than 50 percent per year), the ROI that a private equity group seeks (between 25 and 35 percent) and the ROI that a large company may seek (some are at 15 percent per year) from a potential business acquisition. The difference often takes business sellers – and even M & A firms – by surprise, but it makes perfect sense when you take risk into account.

Although some acquirers speak in terms of multiples of earnings when they discuss pricing a business, in the end it all comes down to future earnings and how much of those earnings are available as a payback on the initial investment. Return on investment (or return on equity) is a method of measuring that payback and involves forecasting the cash flow of the acquisition compared with the initial investment and calculating the rate of return.

For example, we once estimated the value of a product line for which the most likely acquiring candidate would be a large company. Large companies typically have a fairly low cost of capital. They can raise money by selling stock or they can raise money using debt. An average of these sources is called the weighted average cost of capital, or WACC. When a company looks at a project, they often compare the rate of return to their internal cost of raising money – their WACC. If a project returns more than the WACC, it is considered a good investment, since the company can make more money with the project than it costs to get the money. A typical WACC for a large, mature company in a low-risk area can be 8 or 10 percent.

However, risk raises the required ROI significantly. Private equity groups (PEGs) typically require 25 to 35 percent per year return on their investment (which, interestingly enough, often equals about a five times multiple of EBITDA). PEGs typically invest in mature, fairly stable profit-generating companies, as compared to venture capitalists (VCs) who invest in early stage, often pre-revenue, companies. VCs require 50 percent or more per year.

The difference is the risk. In fact, trained business appraisers will "build up" the discount rate (essentially ROI) used for valuations. They'll start with the low-risk discount rate – very similar to what a large, stable company uses – and add risk premiums. There are significant risk premiums added just by the fact that a company is small. In some high-risk tech areas, they end up with a 50 percent discount rate after all the risk factors are added in.

That discount rate is applied to future estimated cash flows. A high-risk technology venture with huge future potential cash flows will be discounted heavily because of the risk premium associated with that industry. It makes sense when looked at as a portfolio. Some tech ventures have enormous payoffs (think Apple, Google and Cisco), but most don't. The high fliers cover the losers so the portfolio still makes a positive return. By requiring a 50 percent ROI, the venture capitalists make sure that the upside is possible.

Private equity groups have an interesting multi-layer business model. They generally raise money from wealthy individual investors or institutional investors (or larger PEGs or sometimes even their family), and typically try to produce an ROI of 15 to 20 percent for these investors. However they seek opportunities that produce 25 to 35% on their investment. The difference, of course, is how the PE fund managers make their money. Some managers will charge an annual management fee, some will charge deal origination fees, but in the end their success is measured by how much they make for their investors.

Typically PEGs try to exit an investment in three to seven years, although some funds will hold longer. Some have very specific timelines they have advertised to their investors, and these funds definitely feel pressure to exit a business at the end of a fund's life. If successful (the fund investors realize 15 to 20% return on investment), the fund managers are much more likely to be able to raise money for future investments. If they are not successful they risk not being able to raise additional money and having to exit the private equity market.

Datapack Offer

Typically the buyer will not want the seller to see their ROI models for obvious reasons (quite simply, they don't want to show their hand). However it is interesting to look at some examples so you can see a deal from the buyer's perspective. I have included in the datapack a couple of ROI Excel models from buyers. One is from a large strategic and the other from a private equity group looking to raise money for an acquisition of my client. You can email me at ney@woodbridgegrp.com for a copy of the datapack.

Confidentiality

Deal Extracts

Where's the Leak?

Leaks are rare so I hesitate to tell a leak story. But it does occasionally happen…

We sold a steel fabrication plant in the California central valley and, although we had a purchase agreement in place and ready, we were waiting for funding. We recommended the seller not disclose the sale to his employees yet, especially since the buyer had some issues with funding.

The first crisis came up when a bank manager, also a friend of the family, asked the seller's 10-year-old-daughter, in front of her young friends, why her father was selling his business. Then two employees approached the owner, asking if he was selling.

Since the word appeared to be out, we developed a plan to announce that sale discussions were taking place. We didn't announce that the sale was complete, as we still had to secure funding and there was always a possibility it wouldn't happen. We don't recommend lying, but sometimes you can leave information out. Employees will often feel betrayed by a lie, but more understanding if you are not forthcoming. You can also dodge the question with a joke ("Hey, you know me, I'm always for sale for the right price."), but don't lie.

The owner was angry and asked who we had told, indicating he thought we were to blame. I assumed it was the bank manager or the young friends, since these were the known leaks. A few days later the owner sheepishly admitted that he had told a few "trusted" employees and then a few more, about five in total. It turned out one of them couldn't keep a secret. The deal did close, and the final sale was announced at a BBQ lunch with both seller and buyer present.

Maintaining confidentiality is usually important in keeping the business healthy while going through the long sales process. Until there is a finished deal to announce, word of an impending sale can spook employees, customer and suppliers. Most business intermediaries are well-trained in how to sell and market a business while preserving confidentiality. Occasionally stuff happens, but I've witnessed close to 100 businesses changing hands with very few problems in this area. All it takes is a good business intermediary who follows an established process and stays aware of problem areas where leaks can occur.

How do you market a company and keep it confidential?

For small or large businesses, the key is to create a campaign with a description that is enticing, but doesn't include enough information to identify the company. To hide a company's identity, sometimes we'll make the location fuzzy (for example "West Coast" instead of "San Diego"). Or we may include the city name, but call it an aviation manufacturing firm instead of the more detailed description of aircraft seat belt manufacturing. We always work with the business to make sure the owners are comfortable with the level of confidentiality of the blind marketing materials before we send them out.

Moreover, maintaining confidentiality is not difficult when dealing with professional investors and other companies as buyers, because they know the ground rules. It is actually much more difficult with small mom-and-pop companies where individuals are buyers – because they often do their own research and naively break confidentiality. Breaches can occur, but they are rare.

Should you tell your employees?

I started and grew a technology company in the late 1990s, and sold it after being approached by a larger public company. From letter of intent to closing it took about six months and, during that time, I let the employees know what was happening. Would I do that again? No, I wouldn't, and I now tell my clients to think carefully before letting their employees know.

Why? One of my employees said it best. After the sale, she admitted that she had had her resume on the street before the deal had closed and was looking for another job. She said she felt like she could no longer completely trust me to keep her safe, because even though I was staying around, I would no longer be fully in control. Fear, uncertainty and doubt spread through the company. The employee said it was a big relief after the deal closed to finally meet more people from the other company and find out they weren't ruthless managers out to cut the operation to the bone. I know that not all the employees were as anxious as this one, but it is natural for your staff to have concerns. It isn't uncommon for some jobs to be cut in an acquisition, whether it is because of redundant departments (such as accounting or human resources) or because it's a good excuse to trim back a little.

Another issue is that you don't really know if a deal will close until it is closed. Every business intermediary who has been around a while has experienced this fact first hand. There are many reasons a deal might not close, such as a financing issue, or an illness. So disclosing a sale to employees can cause a lot of fear and anguish for no reason, and can even damage the company if the word gets out to customers or competitors.

It can be tough to keep the secret, and it can take some creative storytelling. For example, if asked, you can say you are exploring a strategic relationship with another company. After all, an acquisition is a strategic relationship.

You also need to be prepared to have your cover blown. Once we had a deal, but were having trouble getting the buyer financing and we approached the current business owner's bank to get funding. The owner's bank representative found out from the bank, walked into the owner's business and said, "Hey Bob, I hear you are selling!" In that case, only one other person heard, so Bob pulled her aside and explained the deal wasn't done, she had a job if it did sell, etc. Then he implored her to help keep it a secret for a while longer until funding was lined up. That worked, and he announced the deal to the rest of the company about two weeks before close.

I've shown up to visit a business owner and he has already paved the way with some subterfuge. He'll say, "OK, if anyone asks, you are my insurance agent," or "You are my wife's friend." Both have happened to me, and I just went in hoping I didn't get some tough questions. I prefer they say I'm a business consultant, because that fits, and when I show up again with prospective buyers they are not wondering why his wife's friend is back with more people in tow.

Key, trusted employees are different, and it can actually be helpful to have them on your side in an acquisition. Often, an acquisition means growth opportunities for them, so it doesn't hurt to let them in on your plans. Just let them know how important it is not to discuss the plans with other employees.

Business brokers to Investment Bankers: Fees and Services

A business intermediary is a company or person that facilitates the transfer of business ownership from one party to another. Under this catch-all umbrella are commercial real-estate agents, business brokers, merger and acquisition (M & A) advisors and investment bankers, among others.

Business brokerage is generally regarded as working with companies that are valued under $1 million, or with fairly simple transactions over $1 million, such as gas stations and grocery stores. Investment banks work only with very large companies, typically public companies valued at more than $100 million. There is a lot in between, and this middle ground can be broken out in the table.

Business Intermediary	Size of Business (Earnings)
Main Street business broker	Up to $500,000
Upper Main Street business broker	Up to $1 Million
M & A advisors	Above $1 million
Investment bankers	Above $20 million

This book is intended for companies over $1,000,000 in earnings.

Business brokerage

Business brokers generally deal in "Main Street"-type businesses – the sub shops, mailing centers, franchises and strip-mall businesses that drive much of our economy.

Some characteristics of these firms:

Asset Sales

Most small company sales are asset sales (the assets are sold, rather than the stock of the company), and many firms are not comfortable with the complexities of a stock sale. In fact, most states require a FINRA securities license to execute a stock sale.

Web-based Marketing

Brokers use the web to market their listings by using the main business-for-sale websites (which usually cost $50 per month for a membership). Good firms go beyond simple web listings and use other internet and web marketing techniques (Google advertising and photo-based listings can cost over $2,000 per month). Either way, these firms generally aren't versed in the customized marketing often required for selling a larger company.

Simple Transactions

Most small firms do not have the education or the experience to analyze and creatively structure deals that can benefit both the buyer and seller.

Simple Packaging

Brokers typically use the real estate model of preparing and packaging their client companies – they prepare a one or two-page listing and use that, as well as tax returns.

High Volume

A successful firm is a one that requires a decent inventory of listings – typically a minimum of seven to 10. Power brokers will have more than 20, using a young associate to do the legwork of working with buyers. With this many listings, a broker can't afford to spend much time with each business owner.

Lacks Strategic Planning Expertise

Brokers are great at selling Main Street businesses, but generally lack the skill or patience to give a company long-term, value-maximizing advice. Some firms don't like to call themselves business brokers, but a quick look at their inventory of listings will reveal what types of businesses they serve. .

Merger & Acquisition Firms

Some characteristics of M&A professionals:

Asset and Stock Sales

Even large companies structure many of their acquisitions as asset purchases, so M & A firms are usually adept at doing both types of transactions.

Custom Marketing Programs

M & A firms typically market to strategic acquirers and/or private equity groups (professional investors). However, for many mid-sized companies the web is still a great place to advertise, via a blind listing that protects the company's confidentiality. For example, a company producing $500,000 in earnings is just starting to be attractive to some private equity groups, yet is still well within the range of a high net-worth individual who seeks opportunities by searching the web.

A true blend of marketing programs from a company that understands both types of marketing is required to sell mid-sized companies for full market price. On the other hand, larger investment banks that have industry-specific practices (for example, a "retail team" or an "oil and gas team") can add valuable knowledge and contacts. These types of companies will charge $100,000 or more for an engagement and are usually relevant only for larger companies. But some of their contacts can lead to a successful acquisition.

Complete Business Summary

M & A firms typically put together full business summaries including financial analysis, typically called a Confidential Business Review (CBR), Selling Prospectus or simply "The Book" among other names.

A CBR helps greatly in providing an in depth picture of the company to prospective buyers so they don't waste a seller's time with a lot of redundant questions.

Broker and advisor regulations and licensing

Most states require business intermediaries to be licensed, whether you sell small businesses or large. Small business sales are regulated by the state's department of real estate. Large business sales are regulated by the Financial Industry Regulatory Authority and intermediaries must have a FINRA license and the firm must be a broker/dealer. It isn't quite this simple, but the basic difference is that a business broker typically sells the assets of a business, while an M & A firm can sell the stock.

It is important to make sure a firm is licensed, but the license doesn't mean they are actually qualified. Neither the real estate exam nor the stock broker Series 7/79 exams are particularly relevant to selling businesses. More relevant are experience, industry training and additional industry-specific certifications. In other words, check to make sure any firm you work with has the license, but also ask if they are committed enough to the profession to have received other training and certification. For brokers, the IBBA (International Business Brokers Association) has great training programs and a CBI (Certified Business Intermediary) certification that actually has meaning. For M&A professionals, there is the M&A Source organization and ACG (Association for Corporate Growth).

Commissions and fees
Up-Front Fees

Paying an up-front fee really depends on the size of the company – business brokers handling a small company generally don't charge an up-front fee, while firms representing large ones do. However there is a fairly large fuzzy area in between – and here is a guide on how to figure it out.

If you are a small business with earnings less than $500,000, then you would probably approach a "Main Street" broker to sell your business. It is industry standard practice for a broker to not charge an up-front fee. Actually, in many states in which business brokerage is regulated under the department of real estate, brokers are not allowed to collect up-front fees that are a part of the sales commission. If they do charge an up-front fee, it has to be for a tangible product or service such as a formal valuation (not a 5 or 10 page "broker's opinion of value") or serious marketing effort (beyond web listings).

So that is pretty clear – if you are small and use a broker, no fee. It is also pretty clear that if your company has $1 million or more in earnings, you will want to use an M & A firm or investment bank and you will not only pay a up-front fee, you also may have to pay a monthly retainer (however, usually for very large companies).

In the middle ground, it really isn't clear what is what. Business brokers may call themselves mergers and acquisitions advisors and M & A advisors may call themselves investment banks. Some high-growth companies with $500,000 in earnings may well need a good M & A advisor because of the complexities of the business, while a car wash with

$750,000 in earnings may easily be sold by a business broker with no up-front fee.

When paying an up-front fee, be sure to ask what exactly you are paying for. Here are some examples of items you should not mind paying an up-front fee for:

- A professionally-prepared selling prospectus (the book). By the way, there is a big difference between a professionally prepared book and the fill-in-blanks template that some firms use.

- Sales and marketing materials. These include executive summaries, photos, videos, blind web summaries, and letters of introduction.

- Marketing research to uncover strategic and financial buyers. Good research entails using many resources and is very time consuming. It consists of more than running a list based on SIC or NAICS codes. There are subscription services available to do online research of companies on both a national or international basis. These tools are a valuable asset in identifying acquisition activity of buyers and sellers, date of the acquisition and often even how much was paid. The annual fees to subscribe to these kind of databases are often prohibitive for a small firm.

- Actual marketing costs of mailings, telemarketing, etc.

What you don't want to pay for with your up-front fee are commissions to salespeople. Some firms pay up to 50 percent of the fee to salespeople to sign you up, and that is money that isn't being used to prepare and market your company. What's worse, often those same salespeople are the ones who have authority over whether to take you on as a client, creating an incentive to say all the right things to sign you up and get the fee. However, they are not actually responsible for selling your company.

This business model has led to the rise and eventual collapse of some large M & A firms, most notably the Geneva Group. There are similar companies out there today, often using telemarketing and a seminar or web-seminar strategy.

The best thing you can do is ask directly about how the up-front fee and commissions work. Where does that money go and what is it used for? I was in Brazil and the prospective client really drilled me about fees and commissions. He was focusing on the flow of money and where the incentives would be in my firm. That kind of questioning rarely happens in the US, but in my opinion it should occur more often.

Commissions / Success Fees

Business brokers usually charge a 10 percent commission on the value of the business and 6 percent on any associated real estate. We have heard of some brokers charging 12 percent and others readily dropping a few points to get a deal, but most hold firm at 10 percent. It is standard practice to provide a discount above $1 million, and many brokers will say they use the Lehman Scale, although, in reality, they probably use the Double Lehman Scale. If another broker is involved in finding a buyer, the fee is sometimes split between the buy-side broker and the sell-side broker.

Lower middle market M & A advisors typically use the Double Lehman Scale, although there are many variations on this (e.g. Reverse Lehman, Standard Lehman Plus, etc.). The Double Lehman Scale pays 10 percent on the first million, 8 percent on the second million, 6 percent on the third million on down, to 2 percent for the remainder.

M & A firms like Woodbridge International that typically sell companies valued at more than $5 million skip the Double Lehman and use a simplified calculation, but in the end it is similar to the Double Lehman, or will have a fixed dollar amount and an incentive percentage of sale value above an agreed upon target value.

Business brokerage deals often have a clearly defined value and a success fee is fairly easy to determine. Not so with larger, more complex deals, where it is often up to the seller and the intermediary to sit down at some point and figure out a fair commission. A recent deal we closed had a contingent payment based on the future performance of the company – therefore, the full purchase price would not be known for a couple of years. The "expected" purchase price used for commission calculation ended up being above the base price but below the maximum price.

We have a buyer for your business! (Not)

At the lower end of the market, many business brokers send out postcards or invitation cards, often using computer-generated "handwritten" fonts. In the middle market, business owners get first class letters or phone calls. In almost all cases the message is the same: "We have a buyer for your business." Do they have a buyer? Almost never. To be fair, many brokers do have buyers at any given time, so it is remotely possible one of those buyers will be interested, but that's usually not the case.

Typically, the business is sold using business-for-sale websites. The broker is hoping the business owner will call, and that will open up a conversation about selling the company. Often, it is purely about having that card arrive at the right time – when the business owner is starting to think about selling.

Many business owners get lots of these mailings and are used to hearing about all the buyers waiting to buy their business. We've done business searches for wealthy buyers, and we have a heck of a time convincing business owners that we *really do* have a buyer interested in their business.

The marketing for larger companies is often similar. The letter may be on watermarked letterhead with first class postage, but the message is the same. In fact, I was at an industry conference and at the exhibition there was a company that does mailings for firms. The letter looks like it is from a nationwide investment firm and it is pretty impressive. It indicates, in a fuzzy sort of way, that there are buyers who have inquired about "companies like yours." Anyone who responds is sent to the local M&A firm that paid for the mailing.

Some firms also use telemarketing, but use a similar message. Some are starting to use web advertising (we do). Seminars are used, in ways both good and bad. Many use seminars to educate, hoping they impress the attendees enough that they elect to use the company. Some however, use seminars to do a hard sell.

Business-for-sale seminars

I've led sell-your-business seminars and I may do it again someday. The seminar is a common marketing channel that many of us in this industry use. I didn't especially like the travel and set-up, but, once in the room, I enjoyed educating the attendees and correcting common misconceptions. The seminar is a marketing tool, so I would follow up with each attendee to see if we could help them sell their business. But it wasn't a hard sell, and I didn't rush anyone.

However, there are some seminars out there designed to sign up sellers quickly. In fact, I just had a client send me an email announcement about an upcoming seminar – and I happen to know it is one of the bad ones. Like any scam, the best way to attract customers is to tell them what they want to hear. In this case, the company tells the audience that they can unlock the value in their business. Indeed, if the business owner signs up (typically for $20,000 to $50,000), the company provides an inflated valuation that continues to make the business owner happy – for a while. What the business owner doesn't get is a buyer for their business.

For example, this is the text from one seminar:

> **Seminar Flyer Text:**
>
> *"Don't Fall Victim to Using Formulas*
>
> *Many business owners mistakenly base their company's value solely on past performance, rather than on future projections. Our proven M&A process first uncovers each company's unique, often overlooked features. These distinctive qualities cannot be computed by a formula, yet are vital to negotiating the best deal. With this information, we can then build a growth projection incorporating the full scope of your company's strengths.*

The result is an enhanced value for the business, one that could not be predicted by any single formula."

While true in some respects, the seminar company builds on this statement to overvalue and set unrealistic expectations for most business owners. We were called last year by a business owner who went to this seminar. He paid his money and got a wildly inflated valuation. It was based on a growth projection that was clearly unrealistic, since his sales numbers had been in decline and nothing had happened to change that. I asked how he came up with the projection and he said the M & A company had done the projections. It is still hard to believe that they actually did the projections for him, but in any case it was clear the numbers were inaccurate. This business owner called us because the firm had, as far as he could tell, done nothing to sell the business. They had not dug up even one prospect.

The other problem with seminars is that the folks running them are usually paid based on the number of people they sign up and get an upfront fee from, and not on selling companies. An excellent thing to do when you talk to an M & A firm is to ask and understand how people are being paid. Really – go ahead and ask, they should be able to honestly tell you.

Many business-for-sale seminars are good. So feel free to attend, but keep a few things in mind. Don't sign up for anything right away. Go back and do some research (for example, I happen to know that at least one company has more than few entries at ripoffreport.com), and, most importantly, ask for references. A good idea for references is to make sure the M & A firm not only provides past success story clients, but also gives you a reference of someone who is a current client. Even the worst M & A company can accidentally sell a few companies.

Choosing a business broker / M & A advisor

Selling your business is likely to be one of the most important events in your life, so don't just sign up with the first intermediary you find. As with all professions, there are good and bad intermediaries and M & A firms out there. Here are some steps you can take to make sure you are working with someone who will competently guide you through the process of selling your business. (Remember, this book is focused on the middle market.)

1. **Check references from recent transactions.** Selling your business can be a long, arduous process with some tough challenges and conflicts to work through. Contact a couple of the firm's clients and discuss these areas with them:

   - **Integrity** – Did the firm act with professional integrity and give honest, objective advice? Were they willing to deliver bad news as well as the good?

   - **Knowledge** – Did the firm have a good understanding of accounting and financial principals throughout the transaction? Did they take the time to learn about your business?

   - **Persistence** – Not all deals proceed smoothly, so it can take persistence to get a deal done. Did the M & A firm stick with the marketing and work diligently throughout the process?

   - **Communication** – Did the firm's employees communicate well orally and in writing? Did they keep the client informed through the process? Review a sales prospectus as part of your selection process.

   - **Marketing is critical in the middle and lower middle market.** The best price and the best deal structure come from having multiple buyers competing for your business. It is really as simple as that, and it amazes me how many middle market M & A firms don't understand that. It is less important for small companies with a tighter range of possible values (plus they are local and also can't afford an aggressive marketing program). For large companies with a limited number of possible buyers, a wide-reaching marketing program isn't needed. Mid-sized companies, however, directly benefit from marketing because statistics show that, about 75 percent of the time in these middle market deals, the seller didn't know the buyer prior to the deal. In the middle market, using the web and making a dozen phone calls isn't enough.

- **Don't rush in.** Take time to get comfortable with the firm. A quality firm will give you an opinion of value before asking for a representation agreement. There is no need to pay for anything before you have an idea of where you stand and if you really want to sell. A quality firm doesn't want a client who is not committed to the process. It only creates frustration on all sides.

- **Check a list of current engagements.** You might also want to check the size of companies this firm represents to make sure it matches yours. There are plenty of business brokers that would love to attract a larger client by calling themselves "Mergers and Acquisition" advisors. They are hoping to land a big fish, but if you check their listings, it will become apparent that they really handle smaller businesses.

- **Get comfortable with the deal makers.** The deal makers or advisors will be your primary interface for this long and sometimes challenging process. You want to be comfortable with them and with their experience level. It takes at least five to 10 years of full-time deal making to produce the deep and broad experience it takes to smoothly pull off deals. Does your advisor have that? Also does the advisor have a full team behind him or her?

Broker/advisors do more than find a buyer

We occasionally have clients who already have had a buyer contact them or have a list of prospective buyers that we should contact. They want a deep discount on the success fee should we sell to those companies, operating under the assumption that finding the buyer is pretty much all we do. I wish it were that simple. In fact, finding the buyer is often the easiest part of what we do.

Here are a few of the tasks we perform after a buyer is found. It doesn't include what we do before the buyer is found, such as valuation, pricing, analysis, and packaging.

Deal structure guidance

An M & A advisor or business broker has the experience to guide a seller and prevent costly mistakes. For example, a skilled buyer may offer a substantial consulting or employment agreement to a seller. At first glance, most sellers are tempted to take such an offer. This arrangement is in the best interest of the buyer, because he or she is able to deduct the full cost in the year the money is paid, where, typically, goodwill is amortized over 15 years. When you think about it, it is obvious that the cost is not 100 percent salary, but most of it is counted as part of the deal price, and, as such, is deducted from other components of the deal price. Taking a substantial consulting and/or employment agreement is not a good deal for the seller, since the tax rate is ordinary income tax, and not more favorable capital gains. Even worse, there is self-employment tax added on top. In other words, by accepting an offer for a consulting agreement, a seller is losing a significant amount in tax dollars. The point of this example is to show that a professional can help guide a seller through the maze of deal options.

Negotiations – preventing buyer/seller breakdowns

Acquisitions are typically not smooth and it isn't uncommon for deals to fall apart at the last minute because of a disintegrating relationship between buyer and seller. Intermediaries act as buffers, relaying good and bad news and absorbing the harsh first reactions that bad news may elicit. This allows the buyer and seller to maintain a stable relationship.

The M & A Advisor has an Overarching View

The M & A advisor advocates for their client, but often because of our deal experience can take an overarching view that other professionals in the transactions do not. Attorneys are paid to point out the risk in a deal and some (not all) truly do earn the title "deal-killer." When the deal falls apart, and they usually do at some point, the M & A advisors are often the only ones in the transaction who can stand above it all and work toward a reasonable solution to bring the deal back together.

Deal Extracts

We had a deal at one time that took an excessively long period of time to complete. While the deal was in progress the economy faltered, the company was never able to successfully hit their projections and to boot, once we did get a signed LOI and a buyer moving toward closing there were environmental issues with the property that needed further explanation. Two and half years into it and just 24 hours from closing, I got a call from the attorney telling me that an" insurmountable issue had occurred". You can imagine my reaction! We had been through countless meetings, and resolved equally as countless issues and were within 24 hours of closing. Certainly at this point there was not going to be anything that was 'INSURMOUNTABLE!"

As it turned out, our client 24 hours before closing had heard from his fourth largest client that they were going to honor their current contract, however when that ran out in the next few months they would not be negotiating any new business with our client. The company would lose some substantial revenue.

First off, our client absolutely did the right thing and notified his deal t. For every problem there is a solution and to make a long story short. The deal closed in 48 hours instead of 24 while an agreement of new terms was negotiated and drafted to account for this change. My client still wanted to sell and the buyer still wanted to buy, it was just the final hurdle that had to be crossed and there was no reason to say the issue was insurmountable.

Financing

Without financing, most deals wouldn't happen. M & A advisors typically have a network of contacts for both debt and equity, and I've personally spent months helping a buyer find financing. At the end of the process, I've had buyers and sellers say they had no idea of the work involved. I only wish it was easier to convince them of that at the start.

Taxes and Deal Structuring

Deal Extracts

C Corporations are a challenge to sell. Buyers usually prefer to buy the business assets out of the C Corporation, leaving the seller with two levels of taxes – one at the corporation level on the sale and the other when the owner takes the sale proceeds out of the corporation as wages or dividends. It is much better for the seller to sell the entire corporation (in other words, sell the stock). Buyers usually push to buy assets, but often a stock sale is better for the buyer too.

I happened to have sold several private fire-fighting companies. The first one I sold was an asset sale, but the company had a large contract with the state of California. It took the owner months to get the contract signed over to the company that had purchased the assets, and then a few months more to have it done correctly. It was a major problem and it happened in the middle of fire season. I learned from that deal, and made sure the buyer on the next deal knew it would be far easier for him to keep the contracts structured as a stock sale. As it turns out, this deal involved a C Corporation so it was better for the seller as well.

It's surprising how many business owners make the important decision to sell, and only later figure out how much they will have to pay in taxes and fees. It is far better to figure it out ahead of time so you have an idea how much cash you'll actually end up with in a transaction. This chapter will provide a very basic overview of taxes. As always, you should consult your tax advisor when contemplating a sale of your business.

If you happen to be a C-Corp have your tax consultant figure out for you the net proceeds of the sale for both a stock sale and an asset sale and you will clearly understand the difference in tax cost. Often the best way to handle the sale of a C-Corp is to let the buyer know up front we are selling a C-Corp and, plain and simple, it must be a stock sale.

Ordinary income vs. capital gains

Much of your effort when selling your business is to move as much value into capital gains and pay capital gains tax, not ordinary income tax. Some business owners put effort into not paying tax at all, but most prefer to stay out of jail.

Long-Term capital gains

The favorable capital gains tax is based on the gain in the value of assets purchased and then sold after holding the asset for at least a year. Technically, it's the long-term capital gains tax rate, but in business sales, practically everything is held longer than a year, so it's often just referred to as the capital gains rate.

Goodwill

Goodwill (which is an asset) is defined as the difference between the purchase price and the price of the hard assets (like inventory, equipment, etc.). Goodwill is taxed as capital gains and can be written off (amortized) over a period of 15 years by the new owner.

Ordinary income

Ordinary income is taxed at a higher rate, so it is usually the goal to minimize components of a deal that are taxed at ordinary income tax rates. You can't get completely away from paying the higher tax rate, but you want to avoid it as much as possible. For example, business buyers will want a non-compete agreement and there will normally be some value assigned to it\. Any value assigned to non-compete agreements and consulting agreements are taxed at the ordinary income rate.

Depreciation recapture

This one is a surprise for many business owners. The IRS allows you depreciate and "write off" assets at a certain rate that helps effectively lower your tax burden. If you later sell those assets for more than what you wrote down, the IRS cries foul and wants you to pay back the tax savings. Say you depreciated some equipment down to $1,000 (book value), but then sold it for $5,000 (fair market value). The government essentially says, "We gave you the tax benefit of writing it down to $1,000, but it turns out to be worth more than that, so pay us back." The depreciation recapture amount of $4,000 is taxed as ordinary income.

Wages

Wages are at the bottom in terms of compensation for selling a company. If a buyer offers the seller a sweet consulting package for 10 years without the seller actually having to show up for work, it really isn't so sweet. Why? Not only does the seller pay ordinary income taxes, but he or she also gets hit for Social Security payments. If the buyer can't afford to pay the entire purchase price up front, it is better to structure the latter payments as a seller note. (Notes defer taxes, and do not lose capital gains treatment of the underlying transaction.)

Asset vs. stock sale

First, don't confuse an asset sale with a distressed sale, where a company is sold for near the fair market value of its hard assets. An asset sale, for tax purposes, means that a deal is structured so the buyer acquires the underlying company assets instead of purchasing the entire corporation (the stock).

In an asset sale, the buyer acquires a specific set of assets, such as inventory, equipment, goodwill, accounts receivable, and accounts payable. Each asset has a tax attribute and you calculate your taxes on how the purchase price is allocated between the assets. The allocation is a negotiation between buyer and seller. The hard assets transferred are stepped up to the purchase price, and the buyer gets to depreciate them using the new basis.

In a stock sale, the entire corporation is transferred (unless specifically excluded in the purchase agreement) to the buyer, including company name, bank accounts, contracts, abilities, etc. The depreciation schedule is also transferred, so a buyer just continues with the same schedule.

In general, the IRS sets up a natural conflict between buyer and seller, which can cause protracted negotiations on the allocation of purchase price. Payments that get favorable tax treatments for a seller will usually create a negative tax effect for the buyer. For instance, goodwill is taxed at the capital gains rate for the seller (good) and depreciated by the buyer, instead of expensing that cost immediately (bad). The consulting contract mentioned above would get taxed as ordinary income to the seller (bad), but the buyer gets to expense those charges right away (good).

Deferring taxes

There a few ways you can defer taxes on the sale of a business, although except for a seller note or an earn-out, most of our clients don't take advantage of these.

Seller notes

Seller notes normally qualify as installment sales with the IRS, so taxes are not due until you receive payment. Many sellers do not wish to take a note for a portion of their business, although often it is required by a lender, and it makes a lot of sense tax-wise.

Earn-outs

An earn-out (performance-based payout) may also be taxed when you receive payment.

Equity buy-backs

It is rather obvious, but if you don't sell all your company and retain some equity, you typically will not pay tax until you sell that share of the business. This actually is not as simple as it sounds, because, in many cases, a seller doesn't actually keep equity. For example, if the company is sold to a strategic acquirer, then typically the entire company is sold. If the company is sold to a private equity group, then the sale is usually structured as an asset sale where a new company entity is set up, and the assets are moved into that shell. Then the seller buys back equity in the new entity. The problem is that this transaction is fully taxable, and the buyback occurs with after-tax dollars. There are some strategies that can help, and it is essential to get expert tax advice with buybacks. One strategy we have used is to undervalue the equity in the new entity by the use of debt to depress the book value of new equity.

Tax-free mergers

If you take stock in a company for a substantial part of the consideration, then you wouldn't pay tax on the gain until you sell that stock. So really, they should be called "tax deferred mergers" and not tax-free mergers. There are a lot of rules and regulations regarding tax-free mergers and when stock can be sold, so it's best to get tax advice early on.

Structured sales

With the IRS not allowing tax deferral with a private annuity trust, an entirely new industry has popped up around structured sales. These are ways to use an insurance company to set up an annuity, which is only taxable when you receive the money. To use structured sales, you have to set the process up well before the transaction. A key to the tax deferral is that you cannot receive money from the transaction. (Because then, the IRS essentially says, "You've got the money now, so you pay the tax now.") It has to go directly to the life insurance company. The good news is that you get to specify a payment schedule, and it can be just about anything you want. The bad news is that you can't change the payment schedule once it starts.

Charitable remainder trust

Another popular tax deferral method is a charitable remainder trust (CRT). This one is especially nice if you actually have a charity you would like to support. A CRT is an irrevocable, life-time trust that pays out to you at a rate based on current interest rates and a 10 percent minimum remainder goes to your charity of choice when you die. Investment vehicles you can use within the trust are pretty flexible and there are a variety of schemes for the payout, including a fixed percentage of account balances.

The letter of intent explained

A letter of intent (LOI) is non-binding except for a few terms. The most notable of these is the agreement between parties that they will keep everything confidential ("non-disclosure clause") and the agreement by the seller that they will break off talks with all other parties ("no-shop" or "stand-still" clause) for a period to allow the buyer time to conduct due diligence.

For the most part, the LOI is non-binding and either party can back out for any reason. It is uncommon for that to happen because, at this point, both buyer and seller have spent significant time and money in the courtship phase leading up to the LOI. But it happens, and can go both ways. The last time it happened to me it was my client, the seller (actually the seller's wife) who decided at the last minute not to sell. It was a personal decision relating to a family matter, but frustrating nonetheless. I had to make the difficult call to the buyer, who at that point had spent tens of thousands of dollars on due diligence and was ready to close.

The LOI defines what a deal may look like, and then allows both parties (but mainly the buyer) some time to perform due diligence to verify the information presented. It is also used as a roadmap for the attorneys when they craft the final purchase agreement and other closing documents. It is important for an LOI to have enough detail so there isn't a lot of negotiating left to do on major deal terms. There is always going to be some negotiating, but you really don't want to have to deal with something so major that it impacts the overall value of a deal.

The obvious items, price and structure, are pretty hard to leave out, but we've seen some other basic items overlooked. Here are some other examples that should be in the LOI:

- If there is a seller note, the LOI should contain the terms of the note and what, if any, security is on the note. If it isn't a straight note, then a payment schedule as an exhibit can be helpful. For example, was that 2013 balloon payment at the beginning or end of 2013?

- Legal structure (asset or a stock sale).

- If there is an earn-out (future performance-based compensation), then there should be detail on how that is actually earned. If there is any confusion at all, examples can be included to show how any formulas would actually work.

- Unless the seller is going away immediately, which is very rare, there should be details on future compensation for the seller.

- The status of the accounts receivable, payables, cash, etc. and any net working capital requirement should be very clear.

- Often we do deals that include continued ownership for the seller. The structure to make that happen can be complex, and, in that case, it should be clear what the new ownership is. A new ownership table ("cap table") as an exhibit can be helpful to include in the LOI.

Each LOI is different, and is based on the concerns of both buyer and seller. Let's say we have a seller who worries that a buyer will mess with the compensation structure of the company's top salesperson during the seller's earn-out period. We might go to the buyer and ask that a clause be added that states the buyer will provide an employment agreement to this employee that sets the compensation. You can do this after an LOI and before close, but it is usually easier to get in the LOI.

While due diligence is going on, attorneys will take boilerplate purchase agreements, and similar documents and modify them to include terms in the LOI. A four or five page LOI can't possibly include all details of an acquisition or investment, so there are points and issues to resolve. Usually, these are resolved quickly and amicably. Some items are a little more challenging to figure out, but, at that point, buyer and seller are committed to a deal and able to compromise on a solution. Once due diligence is complete, and the purchase agreement and other documents are done, there is really only one thing left: Closing.

Earn-outs

Deal Extracts

We had a client whose revenue was mostly from government contracts in the SBA 8(a) program based on their status as a small, veteran-owned business. Although small is relative because with their industry classification they were at $38 million in sales and still were able to be classified as "small". These contracts grew each year as the government granted them "modifications," which provided additional revenue without actually having to bid for new contracts.

The value of the business was grounded in the future value of the contracts. However, the seller had been working hard on some new contract modifications that would start to create additional revenue over 12 to 18 months. The buyer, on the other hand, was concerned that one or more of the contracts would be re-bid by the government once they found out the business was being sold.

The resulting deal consisted of three components: cash, a seller note and an earn-out. A percentage of the note was contingent on the simple condition that a certain number of the contracts still existed one year after close. This provided protection to the buyer on the contract risk.

The earn-out was based on revenue goals, estimated using the expected contract modifications. This allowed the seller to be paid for the hard work of developing the relationships and the negotiations already done for the future modifications.

What are earn-outs?

An earn-out is a contingent future payment based on performance milestones. For example, in a simple earn-out arrangement, an extra payment of $100,000 to the seller may be "earned" by growing the company by an additional $1 million in revenue in the first 12 months after the close of the transaction. Earn-outs are used when there is a difference of opinion on what the earnings will be in the future. The buyer says, essentially, "Show me." They are also used to protect against risk like high customer concentration.

Some of my clients tell me they would never accept an earn-out, but go on to say how they believe the historical earnings don't tell the whole story and that a buyer needs to believe the company will grow in the future. In other words, the buyer should pay more. Unfortunately, many buyers will say, "I don't quite believe it. Prove it." That is what an earn-out is intended to do – let the seller prove the company's value. Here is how to tell if an earn-out makes sense when you sell your business.

Business are bought for future earnings

In looking at earn-outs, it is useful to remember that what a buyer really cares about are future earnings. Since we don't know what future earnings will be, we generally use historical earnings for valuation. Earn-out discussions naturally arise when there is a significant difference between historical earnings and future projections.

Let's look at a few scenarios of historical vs. projected earnings.

Scenario 1 – stable earnings

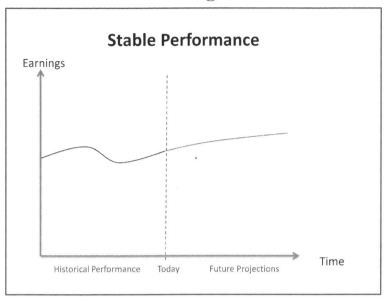

This company has a stable history and a believable projection. In other words, the risk is fairly low, and the seller should not expect an earn-out.

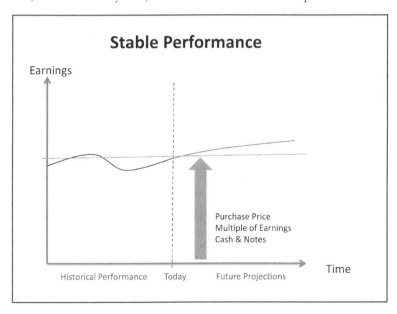

The purchase price in this case should be comprised of cash and possibly a note, but unless there are other risks, the note shouldn't be contingent on revenue or earnings, and generally there should not be an earn-out.

Scenario 2 – supported growth

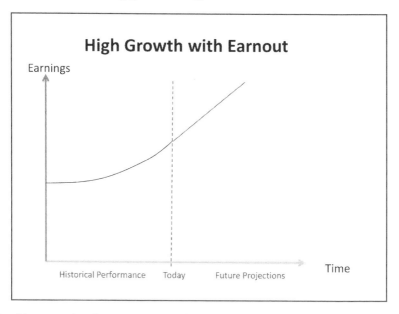

In this scenario, the projection of future growth is clearly supported by historical trends. However, there is often discussion about who is going to benefit from the growth. A seller may say, "You can see what will happen, so I want to base the purchase price on a high multiple, or possibly use next year's earnings."

But a buyer may say that if the company grows, it will be because of his efforts after he buys the company – not because of anything the seller has done. After all, he certainly isn't buying it to give all the earnings to the previous owner.

A smart seller will counter this by explaining that much of the future growth is because of the foundation he has built. The website, reputation, product, service, and other components have all come to together to build momentum that would be difficult to stop. However, what he is also saying is, "Just trust me on this." No one likes to bet hundreds of thousands – or millions – trusting someone they recently met, so earn-out discussions start.

In this type of scenario, an earn-out could look like the following:

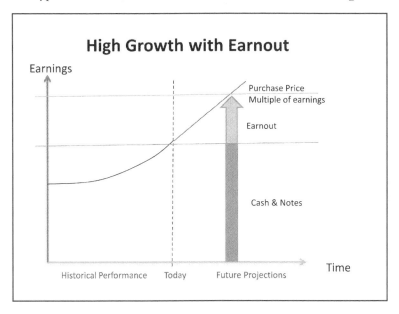

A "base price" of cash and notes is calculated using historical performance, and an earn-out is structured based on the company hitting certain targets. The target may be a revenue or earnings milestone or just about anything that makes sense.

Scenario 3 – unsupported growth

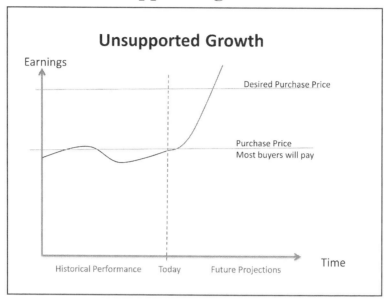

Occasionally we see a scenario where the company doesn't have an obvious upward trend, yet the business owner believes there are a lot of growth opportunities. The owner may say, "I never got around to putting up a website but if you built a website and sold products online, sales would double." Charting this situation looks like the "Unsupported Growth" chart above.

In this case the buyer has a pretty good case to say, "Well, if I spend the money and time to build the website, then I should enjoy the rewards." Sometimes we can negotiate an earn-out in this type of scenario, but it depends on the situation and why exactly the seller believes growth is inevitable.

Scenario 4 – recession-proofing a transaction

Although earn-out agreements are mostly seen in growth companies, we've also seen them used a few times to protect the buyer from further decline during the recession. Many companies have seen a retraction of sales and earnings from the time before the recession, and that is just fine with buyers – as long as the performance has stabilized. We've seen buyers, fearful of further decline, set a purchase price on a lower "base" number, then set up an earn-out target of simply staying put. In other words, if the business does the same in revenue and earnings in the future, then additional payments are made to the seller. If the business slides some more, then the seller gets the "base" price that was somewhat lower.

How often are earn-outs used?

Small businesses generally don't use earn-outs, and for good reason. In small-business transactions, there are typically short transition periods. (Usually sellers "earn" an earn-out by staying during a transition but not always.) Financials are often fairly messy, so measuring earn-out milestones is problematic. Buyers also usually want to come in and operate the business as theirs without any of the operating limitations that often occur with an earn-out arrangement.

However, they are fairly common for larger companies in the lower middle market and middle market. Valuation gaps between buyers and sellers are common, and that naturally leads to discussions on earn-out.

It is also fairly common for earn-outs to disappear later in negotiations when the challenges of actually structuring the earn-out become apparent. Typical issues that need to be worked out include figuring how to measure the earn-out, how long to make the earn-out period and what operational limitations will be placed on the buyer.

For example, I did a deal in which there was initially an earn-out planned. During last-minute negotiations, with two buyers still left bidding, one of the buyers dropped the earn-out and made that payment a non-contingent note. That swung the deal his way and the next day the seller signed that buyer's LOI. It also simplified the purchase agreement that would soon come.

The American Bar Association puts out a deal points study in which they organize deal information from a number of middle market deals. In 2007, they analyzed 103 deals and 20 percent of those deals had earn-outs structured into the agreements. In 2009, 104 deals were analyzed and 29 percent had earn-outs, which makes sense given the higher volatility and risk of earnings in 2009. Those deals were in the higher middle market between $20 million and $100 million. I believe the percentage is higher for middle market deals at $5 to $50 million.

Earn-out period

In summary, make the earn-out period not too short and not too long. If it's too short, the seller has an incentive to act in a completely short-term manner, possibly playing games with trading long-term revenue with short-term. If the earn-out period is too long, it can delay and impact the integration with the buying company and/or new owner. Earn-out periods of 18 months to three years are the most common, but I've seen them go on much longer. The length of the earn-out also often depends on how long the seller is still involved in the business. Naturally, the seller wants some control of the company during the earn-out period to make sure the company achieves the targets.

According to a 2009 American Bar Association study of 100 middle market transactions, only 4.3 percent of the deals studied had an earn-out period of less than 12 months. About 30 percent had an earn-out last between 12 and 23 months; 36 had earn-out periods of 24 to months and 29 percent of earn-outs took more than 36 months.

Amounts in earn-outs

It is hard to provide much guidance on the amount, since it completely depends on the deal and how much earnings risk the buyer is trying to mitigate. I've done earn-outs ranging from 10 percent of the purchase price to 50 percent of the purchase price, although 20 to 30 percent are more common.

A buyer will commonly wish to base an earn-out on EBITDA because, after all, that is really what he cares about. A seller's most common fear is that, even if he is still around, he will not have complete control over costs and, therefore, can not control EBITDA. Indeed, an experienced deal attorney once told me this is the issue that causes the most lawsuits after a deal is closed. For this reason, we try to negotiate earn-outs based on revenue milestones, not EBITDA. If we fail at that, gross margins can also work. Basically, the further up the profit and loss statement you go, the easier it is to measure earn-out.

Interestingly enough, we had a situation where measuring earn-out as a percentage of EBITDA was the best solution for the seller. In this case, the seller was performing a myriad of tax maneuvers to lower his taxes, and try as I might, I could not convince him to stop for even one year (despite the fact that he would pay 40 percent in taxes, but would receive 400 percent in increased purchase price for each dollar earned). He admitted that all this would end when the buyer bought the company, and then the buyer would receive a windfall because EBITDA would almost magically be higher. So we negotiated an earn-out on an increase in EBITDA, not in revenue or gross margin.

You can also measure earn-out on events such as signing (or often re-signing) a major contract, getting government approval or launching a new product.

Keep in mind that complex formulas based on revenue, gross margins or earnings are problematic when it comes to actually writing a purchase agreement and making sure that, months later, everyone who reads it will come away with the exact same understanding. It's easy to brainstorm and draw graphs and curves, and talk about cliffs and caps. But always keep in mind that you should keep it as simple as possible and that complex algebra doesn't translate well into a legal agreement.

Controls and restrictions

A seller will often say something like, "OK, I'll live with that earn-out based on growth of 15 percent next year, but in return I want some reassurances – in writing." These are some of the restrictions or buyer covenants that are often put into place during the earn-out period:

- Office will stay in same location.

- Key employee(s) will not be terminated.

- Sales compensation structure will remain the same.

- A certain amount of capital will be invested in a project.

However, each restriction is a negotiation in itself, which is another reason to keep everything as simple as possible. For example, it is easy to say that a key employee cannot be terminated, but what if he commits extortion? You can say that sales compensation will remain the same, but maybe the new company uses a different healthcare package. You could argue that this changes the compensation. This issue needs to be addressed and covered in the purchase agreement. In other words, the issues that need to get worked out in earn-outs tend to run much deeper than anticipated. It isn't uncommon for earn-outs to disappear late in negotiations when the parties figure out there are just too many issues to address.

Strategic vs. Financial Buyers

Deal Extracts

We had a great client who received an offer from a strong strategic buyer who saw manufacturing, raw material buying and sales channel synergies. The offer was about six times EBITDA. We were right in the middle of the worst of the recession, so that may seem great. But this company was growing rapidly in an industry favored by the new administration. We (and the business owner) were not too excited with the offer since, at his growth rate, he could realize the same sort of return on his own.

We had a few private equity groups interested, and one of them could see the future growth potential and made a great offer. Eventually, the strategic buyer understood that the deal was getting away from him and indicated that they would come back with a higher offer. We were surprised when we didn't hear from them for a few weeks. The strategic buyer seemed to have everything to gain from this acquisition, but the offer from the PEG beat them hands down. We laughed among ourselves in the office that apparently the axiom that strategic buyer pay more than financial buyers isn't true every time.

However we were a little early with our judgment. Sometimes internal decision making with strategics, especially large ones, can be ponderously slow. The new offer that came in was 12 times EBITDA – a solid offer that would allow the business owner to tap into the buyer's big infrastructure and greatly accelerate his growth. So the axiom remained true in this case.

Strategic buyers

A strategic buyer is an entity that is typically involved in the seller's industry and can enjoy some synergistic benefits from the purchase beyond the face value of the stand alone earnings stream, such as:

- Attaining economies of scale
- Reducing competition
- Exploiting new technologies
- Increasing buyer power
- Expanding geographically
- Filling a weakness in product or service lines
- Providing enhanced opportunities for employees
- Establishing strategic alliances
- Eliminating redundant functions

It is important to remember that, in the end, any acquisition needs to increase earnings for a strategic buyer. Value is always related to earnings. Strategic buyers don't pay a premium automatically. They'll try hard to buy at the lowest possible price (like financial buyers) and it's typically a competitive bidding situation that causes them to increase the bid. The difference is that they know they can often increase the bid because of the extra value derived from synergies.

When selling a business, it is best to assume that there are no stupid buyers, and specifically that strategic buyers will pursue your business at all costs. Occasionally, we'll get a business owner who wants to put his business on the market for substantially more than it is worth. They hope that a strategic will see the unique qualities of their business and pay handsomely for it. For example, I was representing a business owner, and it came to light that some of the company's important contracts were not being renewed. Since the earnings and valuation were based on the income from these contracts, I had to tell him that his business was no longer worth what we thought it was. He didn't like that at all, and was adamant about continuing to hold out for $12 million. .

He brought up every reason he could think of. He pointed out that his was an interesting and unique business. That was true, and that could have meant a premium price – but not 25 percent more value. Then he said that the buyer could replace the lost contracts. That was possible, but, if they did that, then the value created should belong to them. Finally, he said "It is like a house, right? Buyer beware." In other words, he was hoping for stupid buyer to come along.

The problem is that not many strategic corporate buyers are that naïve. It is unlikely that they will ignore the fact that they can't make the payments on debt (almost every individual buyer uses debt) and will likely go out of business. Also, most buyers will eventually turn an advisor such as an M & A firm, CPA, attorney, spouse, or friend. These advisors also would have to be stupid to miss the obvious flaws. Similar to an industrial accident caused by a series of mistakes, it takes a series of stupid people to pull this off. That just doesn't happen often.

The best transactions in business sales are truly win-win, with everything disclosed and at a fair price that allows the buyer to operate and enjoy the business.

Financial buyers and private equity groups

Financial buyers, typically private equity groups (PEGS) or wealthy individuals, are buying strictly on the financial strength of the stand-alone company. They are simply trying to buy low and sell high, usually with a time frame of three to seven years. Financial buyers, as you can imagine, are adept at analyzing the financials, gross margin data, market data, competition and other aspects of the deal – whereas a strategic buyer will often already know many of those details if they are already in the industry.

Typical middle market PE – committed funds

A committed or dedicated equity fund is one where the investors have actually invested capital into the fund. A pledge fund is where investors have pledged to invest if the fund manager finds a suitable investment. A search fund (or dry fund) is where fund managers go out looking for opportunities, then come back to investors, often larger private equity funds, to obtain the capital.

Typical lower middle market PE – search funds

Private equity firms often set a minimum level of EBITDA at $1, 2 or 5 million. Some firms will look at opportunities in the $500,000 range, but often that area is home to smaller search funds.

I once received an email from a business owner who had a letter of intent to sell a majority interest to a private equity group, but he was having second thoughts about how professional the PEG really was. I told him I would do some research. This PEG was not listed in any of our databases. I went to their website, which was obviously new, and they did show one transaction, but I called that business owner and he said they didn't directly execute that transaction. This equity group is made up of two guys looking for smaller deals from $500,000 to $1 million in EBITDA.

This is probably a "search fund" or "dry fund", where they don't actually have money in hand, but get commitments for the funding after they have already located and negotiated an LOI with a company. Some of them work with larger private equity groups. Some have arrangements with wealthy investors, and some use family money. The important thing to realize is that they don't actually have the money, and it is possible they never will. These search funds range from opportunistic sharks, purely acting as deal finders, to trusted industry experts who are as good as gold in terms of raising the funds, and add great value post-transaction.

It is our job to point out the differences, and when, meeting with private equity groups, ask some pointed questions. If you are working with an equity fund, pose the questions listed below:

- Ask them directly who their investors are. Are they private individuals, friends and family, or larger PE funds?

- What is the process and under what conditions do they get the money? Ask for this in detail.

- Try to understand if they have to pitch this opportunity from the ground up to investors, or if they have some latitude in finding certain types of deals.

- Do they plan to use any debt, and if so under what conditions will this happen? Are they dependent on raising debt?

- Be very clear on the terms in the LOI. It is common for private equity groups to present an offer in terms of total value or cash payment, and then mention that the seller would retain equity in the form of an equity buyback. An equity buyback uses some of that cash – sometimes a lot of it.

Remember, you usually want some added value besides their money. If they are industry veterans who can pull together a good board of directors, add key employees and use their knowledge to grow the company, you can both win. That is why it can be important to talk to their references from past deals. This is also why it can be important to get an M & A advisor involved.

We usually bring in multiple offers from PE groups. I have a client now who we did not consider PE material. He is a distributor who carries products from one manufacturer, and that is just too much risk for most professional investors. Still, I had over 100 PE groups take a close look, and we ended up with three offers from private equity. One of these was from a search fund with a relationship with a larger San Francisco-based fund, while two were larger funds.

Why private equity uses debt to leverage its investment

The best way to understand why PEGs use debt is to look an example of what leverage does to investment returns. Let's say you raise a $50 million fund from a couple of your drinking buddies. You tell them you hope to be able to get them 15 percent annual return on their money. Of course, you are hoping to make even more than 15 percent, so you can take home some for yourself. You find an excellent $10 million dollar service company with earnings of $1 million before taxes, interest, depreciation and amortization. You buy that company for five times earnings, and seven years later sell it for the same price, $5 million. (You could have invested more money in the company in order to grow it, but you didn't).

Let's look at some scenarios:

100 percent Cash, No Debt = 11 percent ROI

You figure you have $50 million to spend, and your dad told you to always pay cash if you can, so you don't use any debt at all. You invest $5 million, enjoy $600,000 or so of earnings each year (after tax), and get your money back in seven years. The ROI on this is around 11 percent if everything goes right. Your drinking buddies demand the remaining $45 million back in year one once they realize the investment you made.

50 percent Debt = 16 percent ROI

Let's say you get a simple interest 10 percent balloon acquisition loan based on the assets of the business. Now you invest only $2.5 million, use $2.5 million in debt, and have $450,000 of earnings each year after interest payments and taxes. The return on your investment in this case is 16 percent. Better, but now you have the tough decision to keep some for yourself, or pay everything to your buddies to keep them happy.

80 percent Debt = 33 percent ROI

Now you understand leverage, so you get the seller to carry some paper. You get an asset loan based on the equipment, a credit line based on the accounts receivable and use the stability and cash flow of the company to get a loan with warrants attached. After interest payments and taxes, the earnings are only $360,000, but you only need to put in a little over $1 million (including expenses) of your buddies' money. The ROI in this case is 33 percent. Now you take a healthy cut, and your buddies are happy and want to give you $150 million next time around.

This is obviously a simplistic example, but it does show that leverage works, and quite dramatically. Of course there is obvious risk in having too much debt (too much debt service can kill a company if business slows), so it makes sense to ask each PE buyer about how much debt they intend to use. This isn't quite so much the problem it used to be because generally you can't raise the same amount of debt you could in the 90's and early 2000s.

Due Diligence and Getting to the Finish Line

Deal Extracts

The Ups and Downs of a Deal

Dan and Alice had been in business more than 18 years, renting large emergency response equipment to the U.S. government. We put the business up for sale and generated multiple offers. Several from strategic buyers in the same industry, were not high enough, perhaps because they knew more about the industry than some of the other buyers.

The winning offer was from a wealthy individual with PE backing, and after lengthy negotiations, a deal was struck. The offer was contingent on a number of financial maneuvers involving some real estate and the diversion of a 401K investment into a C-Corporation that could then execute the acquisition. In addition, the selling company was a C-Corporation, which created several tax issues that had to be settled. As the complexity built, the deal seemed mired in insurmountable obstacles. But with a lot of hard work, we slowly knocked down all of the obstacles and were ready to set a closing date.

The purchase agreement and the multitude of schedules had been all but finalized and an appointment had been set for the signing. A week before the close, a very emotional Dan called and said Alice had demanded a divorce the

103

night before, and they can't sell after all. That was a complete surprise, especially since divorce often spurs a sale, rather than killing it. Dan didn't say it, but it occurred to me that the business had actually kept Dan and Alice apart and out of each other's way for years, since they each traveled with different groups of equipment. Now they were looking at a life of being together more.

I made a call to the buyer to let him know it was dead. The selling process spanned more than a year, and it had been in due diligence/financing for about four months. Then a week later, Dan called and said that he and Alice had worked it out, decided to stay married and sell the business. The buyer, thankfully, was still willing to move forward. We closed a short time later.

Completing negotiations and accepting an offer is a huge milestone in the deal process, but generally it means you are only about halfway to completion. Once an offer (typically in the form of a letter of intent) is agreed upon, it's time for the buyer to take a closer look and for the seller to open the books. This is the due diligence period.

Naturally, there is a sense of relief in coming to an agreement on price and deal structure since much of the uncertainty is gone, but it is all too common to relax a little too much at this point. We have seen deals slip away during due diligence, or become unnecessarily rough and rocky. For example, I had one seller who forgot what projections he had shown the buyer previously, and presented an entirely different set of sales numbers during due diligence. Both sets were valid. It was merely a matter of definitions, but the buyer didn't know that and went into panic mode.

What is appropriate due diligence?

Simply put, due diligence is "open book" time, when a buyer gets to investigate a potential acquisition to make sure that the business is in the condition represented by the seller.

Medium/Large Business Due Diligence

Due diligence typically starts with a non-binding letter of intent to purchase. A definitive purchase agreement is typically not created until after due diligence. Due diligence can range from little more than a "book check", to a team of 100 attorneys spending months to research a company. Typically for the middle market it consists of some sort of "quality of earnings" analysis by accounting professionals as well as legal and technical due diligence.

Typically, due diligence will investigate the following areas of a company:

- Financial books and records
- Incorporation documents
- Employee benefits, policies and compliance issues
- Internal systems and procedures
- Customer contracts
- Intellectual property
- Condition of assets
- Environmental
- Customer / vendor interviews
- Review of all business and legal contracts
- Any key area of concern identified while negotiating the letter of intent

Fortunately, many of the items on the detailed due diligence list don't apply in most instances, so you can mark them "NA" for "not applicable" and shorten the ordeal to something more manageable. For example, there may be questions about the condition of real estate but for this transaction there is no real estate involved.

How not to do due diligence

I once sold a business whose assets consisted of a bunch of heavy equipment related to wild land firefighting. The equipment was stored in a remote location in far northern California. The buyer had done his financial due diligence, but needed to take a closer look at the equipment. I told him he had the right to take any of the equipment to a mechanic, but I also offered to personally fly him in with my plane so he could take a look himself. We did the latter, and he spent hours looking at the equipment. Unfortunately he wasn't a mechanic.

The deal closed shortly before the first wild fire of the season, and one of the tractor/trailer units responding to the fire was stopped for a highway safety check by the California Highway Patrol. It didn't pass and the unit wasn't allowed to move until it was fixed. It was actually not a major item, but the new owner felt the immediate impact of not being able to deliver the equipment to the fire on time. Things just went downhill from there between the seller and buyer. Last I heard, they do not speak to each other.

Sometimes it is difficult to collect the material for due diligence. We had a client with an $10 million revenue business that was completely operated from their house. They were not very organized, so my partner and I showed up with a digital scanner and set up shop at the dining room table (we don't always get hands-on for due diligence, but sometimes the seller needs help). We went through the buyer's due diligence list and scanned everything we could in three or four hours. Unfortunately, some very important contracts never turned up, but somehow we worked around that.

It is good to remember that the basic concept of due diligence is that the buyer gets to validate whether the seller was honest about the condition of everything related to the business. I've had more than one instance where, upon closer look, things turned out to be less than represented. In one case, the assets were worth closer to $800,000 than the $1,000,000 that was represented. Usually the seller isn't maliciously trying to mislead. They may have just estimated the number of assets without checking.

Other due diligence issues

Paper or Electronic Deal Room?

A lot of due diligence is done via electronic deal rooms. Fortunately, the cost of these services has come down quite a bit in the last few years. Firms like Firmex or V-rooms are specially built for due diligence and have audit trail capability and nice features like watermarking each document that is downloaded. You can also get by using a cheaper service, such as DropBox or Google Docs. However, we still have clients who have all their documents organized in binders, which can work well too. Normally, in the case of a paper-based system, the buyer will send a team to the seller's site to review and copy the needed documents. Our company subscribes to an electronic deal room service so we can offer unlimited deal rooms to our clients.

Keep the Deal Moving

Delay is probably the most frequent deal killer, and due diligence delays are among the worst. Normally, diligence is 60 to 90 days, but some deals stay in due diligence for six to nine months. The entire process can be tough and can take a toll on everyone involved. You still have to run your company and respond to a lot of requests for information.

Should I Disclose Everything in Due Diligence?

Yes. Your liability as a seller is far less if you disclose rather than hide, especially during the due diligence phase. The only time you would not disclose something is if it is so proprietary that you only wish to disclose it after the sale is completed. For example, Coke probably isn't going to disclose their formula until a deal is actually closed, although a cautious buyer may want the formula held in escrow. Sometimes it matters who the buyer is. Coke may also hold back some marketing plans if a competitor were buying them, but would disclose them to a financial buyer.

The Definitive Purchase Agreement

The purchase agreement is written to address issues discovered in due diligence. For example, perhaps there were some outstanding warranty issues with customers that were discovered, and the buyer has agreed to cover these. The agreement will lay out a structure to handle this (a hold back account, deductions from future payments, price adjustment, etc.).

In the end, there must be some degree of trust

Buying a business isn't like buying a house. With a house, you can examine the foundation, walls and roof, and, of course, hire a house inspector to help you do it. Although there are often some surprises, for the most part you have a pretty good idea of the condition of the house.

Plus, the previous owner moves out, and the next owner moves in – in that order.

You can examine many parts of a business, but often there are some intangibles that are hard to assess – like the ability to continue to land long-term contracts in the future. Also, many businesses we sell require the ongoing involvement of the previous owner for at least a few months, if not for years. That's like buying a house, and then having the previous owners live in the house with you for a few months so you'll know how to operate the A/C, stove and garage door. In addition, often the buyer will still owe the seller money for years to come, even if a bank loan is involved. The transition is less clean cut than most real estate purchases. In the end, there has to be some degree of trust between buyer and seller.

We had a deal fall apart because the "trust gap" was just too large. In this environment, many buyers are cautious, which is fine to a degree. I sure would be. But this buyer offered a very low cash payment for the business (in case it went downhill), and offered to pay everything else as an earn-out over 10 years. In addition, he had some specific ideas of how he would run the company, but considered these ideas proprietary and refused to share them with the current owner.

The current owner had his own trust issues, some well-grounded. Even after meeting the prospective buyer, he wasn't completely convinced that the buyer could adequately run the business. A significant amount of the value would be based on future payments and the ability for the new buyer to run the company. I believe the owner's words were, "I know I can run the company and make a good living, so I would rather bet on me than bet on an unknown." The seller was OK with some earn-out, but not nearly the amount the buyer wanted. Since the buyer refused to share how he would run the company, we were not able to ease the owner's fears.

There are always hurdles to overcome on these deals, but this was too much and I didn't waste much time or energy trying to convince either side. The owner has a great business and I'm sure someone will buy it. If the owner gets comfortable with the buyer, I hope the buyer will be more flexible with the terms. This buyer now wants to look at other companies. If he looks at one of ours, I hope he'll understand that, at some point, it always takes a little bit of trust.

Closing a deal: Moving from negotiations to logistics

At the time of writing this, we are days away from closing a deal. The attorney on our side made a comment that we need to close soon, because the buyer's attorneys were sending back revisions on agreements with nothing but changes in spelling and punctuation. I knew we had crossed the line from negotiations into logistics, but it seems we have gone all the way into the grammar stage. When you are paying your attorneys $400 an hour, a few misplaced commas are OK.

We are stalled waiting for the seller to receive a research contract. The problem is that, once the deal is done, the seller will no longer qualify for the contract. All the attorneys agreed that if he signed the contract before the transaction, it would be a legal contract. So everyone decided to wait for a few weeks to see if the seller could get the federal government to push the contracts through. The feds are apparently expediting the contract, but in the meantime we wait.

Usually the pace doesn't slow like this. There generally comes a time when you spend all of your time on the pure mechanics of getting everything done (such as preparing legal docs, moving over payroll, and conveying contract) instead of negotiating terms, like who pays for sick time owed. Usually the pace quickens until you close. It is a nice change to have everything complete and ready, but the process is nerve-wracking at the same time. My job is to attack delays and make them go away. In this case, there was a very good business reason to wait, but it is still hard to do.

Purchase Agreements

Sample Purchase Agreements – Datapack

This book would be far too long and boring with sample purchase agreements included, however I have "sanitized" the stock purchase agreement and asset purchase agreement from "A Tale of Two Deals" examples and have made them available. I have also written an introduction to these with plain language descriptions of the important sections of a purchase agreement.

To obtain the Datapack, please email me at ney@woodbridgegrp.com and I will send you an electronic copy of the agreements.

A Tale of Two Deals

In one week, we closed two substantial deals. Although only a day apart, these deals were completely different from one another in numerous ways. Below, we'll break down the differences in the two deals, and what they both can teach you about this process.

The asset sale vs. the stock sale

One of these two sales was an asset sale, where specific operating assets were sold to the buyer. The other was a stock sale, where the stock of the corporation (and therefore the entire company) was sold to the buyer. Most buyers prefer an asset sale, and some will even go so far as to refuse to do anything but an asset sale. Here are a few reasons why:

Undisclosed Liabilities are Not Assumed

With an asset sale, only specific assets identified in the purchase agreement are acquired. This means undisclosed and unknown liabilities are not acquired or assumed. In plain English, this means if the seller was dumping toxic waste out the back door, or a lawsuit against the company was about to erupt, the buyer is well protected, since those liabilities stay with the seller. The importance of this is obvious.

In the asset sale we dealt with, the seller was a very clean company with low risk of a nasty surprise, but buyers, especially professional buyers like a private equity group, will automatically go for the asset sale. Why take the risk?

In a stock sale the seller would be liable for undisclosed liabilities that originated before the sale – every stock purchase agreement will contain language to that effect. But, the process is different because a lawsuit for something that happened before the acquisition will probably name the new company, which the buyer now owns. The buyer then can use the purchase agreement to sue the seller.

Flexible Newco Structure

If a buyer purchases stock, they are stuck with the structure of the original company, in this case an S-Corporation. In an asset sale, the buyer sets up a new company of their choosing (usually referred to as Newco during a transaction for the simple reason that the company usually isn't given a formal name until later). This buyer prefers LLCs for all acquisitions, because LLCs can be set up in flexible ways by careful crafting of the LLC operating agreement. For example, one big difference between an S-corp and an LLC is that an LLC can be set up so that profit flows per the operating agreement independent of ownership percentages, whereas with an S Corp the profit flows to the corporate owners by stock ownership percentages.

Asset Sale Boosts Cash Flow by Re-depreciating Assets

This was not a factor in our deal because there were so few hard assets, but typically a buyer wants to do an asset purchase that allows them to pay fair market value for the hard assets, and then depreciate them again. This hurts the seller because the government doesn't allow assets to be depreciated multiple times. So, they will charge the seller normal income tax rates (vs. capital gains rates) on the gain on the assets, as compared to their depreciated or book value. (This is called depreciation recapture.)

Our Deal

Our deal was structured as an asset sale, although it became very complicated for tax reasons related to the equity rollover of the seller's ownership. The main issue we ran into is that, in an asset sale, the customer contracts are between the customer and the original corporation, which isn't being sold. So the seller must get the contracts assigned to Newco in the days before close. Just the mechanics of getting this done can be daunting if there are a large number of contracts. In our case, there were thousands of contracts and the buyer knew that would be an impossible task, so they requested that the top customer contracts be assigned. The top customer was an international customer who had his own timetable on when things got done. It just wasn't a priority for him like it was for us, and you can only push your top customer so much.

Our deal was delayed as everyone waited for the contract to be assigned. We were a little nervous because delays are never a good thing. The sellers were getting quite anxious, for we had been fast approaching the end of a long and winding road, yet now we were stalled. The buyer even had the wire transfer instructions ready to initiate a transfer of the purchase price. Fortunately, the buyer understood that we couldn't push the customer any further and that they were causing some degree of angst at the company. They agreed to close without the contract assignment. We closed. The contract assignment came in the next morning.

Stock sales

A stock sale is what many think of as an acquisition. Similar to buying a house and obtaining a deed that proves ownership, a business buyer buys the stock that proves ownership. The buyer pays the seller, and the seller gives the buyer the actual shares of stock. The corporation continues, now under a different owner. However, there are exceptions to the "everything goes" concept of a stock sale and there are invariably some changes that will occur with the change in ownership.

Why Structure as a Stock Sale?

As I wrote above, most buyers prefer an asset sale, both to avoid undisclosed liabilities, and for tax and cash flow reasons. So, most of the time our acquisitions are structured as asset sales, but there are a few reasons why a stock sale is used, the two most common being:

1. There are too many customer contracts or there are a few large customer contracts that you don't want to change. With a stock sale, the contracts continue with no change (unless the contracts

contain a specific "change of ownership" clause). With an asset sale, the contracts need to be changed or assigned to the new company that purchased the operating assets and often (for instance, with large government contracts) it can be difficult to get them assigned in a reasonable amount of time.

2. If the company being acquired is a C-Corporation, then a stock sale avoids the double taxation issue of an asset sale. With a C-Corporation acquisition structured as asset sale, the proceeds from the sale of the assets flow into the C-Corp. Corporate taxes are paid, but the net proceeds are still stuck in the C-Corp. To get them out, the owners have to take wages or dividends, and thus pay taxes again. It is a painful way to sell a business.

Our Recent Stock Sale

In our recent deal we structured the transaction as a stock sale because our client was (and still is) a C-Corporation. By the way, not all C-Corps can be sold as a stock sale. If there is a history of lawsuits, if the owners played fast and loose with the finances, or if there is an inherent problem with potential liability (e.g. the company installs asbestos floors), then many buyers will just plain refuse to execute a stock sale.

Note to owners of C-Corporations: I try not to audibly groan when a new client tells us they are a C-Corporation. Unless you have a large number of shareholders, there are few reasons to still be a C-Corporation. Visit your attorney and elect to be an S-Corporation. It takes 10 years to become 100 percent free from the pain of double taxation, but every little bit helps.

Our client ran a clean company, but it still took some negotiations to get approval of a stock sale. I had dealt with this buyer on a previous acquisition, an asset sale, and right from the start I told him this needed to be a stock sale. His reply was, "Ney, you know us, and you know we do only asset deals." The key was that another strategic buyer also was extremely interested in our client, and within a week, both of these buyers had agreed to a stock sale.

This intense competition also kept the price up. It isn't uncommon for the price to go down during negotiations for a stock sale, because the buyer is sacrificing cash flow (they lose depreciation on the stepped up value of the assets) and their return-on-investment projections go down.

Getting to the Close

There is always some challenge to closing. In this case, our client learned that they had been awarded a government contract, and that they should expect delivery of the actual contract at any time. The moment the stock deal was signed, it was possible that our client would no longer meet the terms and conditions specified in the contract, so he preferred waiting and signing the contract before close. Similar to the asset sale described above (but for different reasons), we were stuck waiting on a contract.

We finally closed the deal after a few weeks of waiting. For a while, it looked like both deals would close on the same day, which would have been interesting. As it was, the deals closed on consecutive days, which was still a lot of fun.

The strategic buyer vs. the financial buyer

The world is rarely black and white, but with the two deals, one went to a strategic buyer. while the other went to a financial buyer., a classic private equity group with a dedicated fund and intelligent, professional management.

The Strategic Buyer

Our client makes underwater instrumentation to detect vital biological and chemical parameters in oceans and lakes. This is an active area, and it is expected to have a healthy growth rate because of the global concern about the environmental state of our oceans, lakes and streams. It turns out there are some large companies building a foundation for water quality testing and measurement. The companies that were most interested in our client were large companies that already had other types of water quality testing and measurement systems, or complementary technologies, such as the underwater test vehicles that carry the sensors.

The successful bidder was one of the latter. This buyer felt the companies could both increase revenue by using their complementary products and services, and decrease cost by using their purchasing muscle and manufacturing knowledge. The first question that many will ask is, "Did they pay more than a financial buyer would?" It's a little hard to say because the potential and growth rate would command a good price, even from financial buyers. But yes, this buyer likely paid more than a financial buyer would have.

However, a common myth is that a strategic buyer isn't buying financial performance and doesn't pay much attention to the financials. This was the perfect strategic buyer, and yet this buyer was focused on the financials throughout. Make no mistake – it is all about the earnings, even with a strategic buyer. They may be looking at future earnings that are hard to conceptualize at the time, but it is all about the earnings.

While we are a negotiating price with the strategic buyer, the smart ones are not saying, "Gee, we really want this business, so let's pay more." They are running their financial models, calculating return on investment, and figuring out how much they can pay. For some strategic buyers, the analysis may point to synergies. This means they can pay more than a financial buyer. In some cases, however, it means they will pay less. They may know too much!

The strategic buyer is looking at the financials, but is also looking at the synergies. This can result in a busy due diligence period. Whereas a financial buyer usually leaves things pretty much as they are, a strategic buyer typically has to answer a lot of questions. Here are a few:

- How will the sales teams work together?
- How will employees be paid in the short term and the long term, relative to the new company's policies?
- How will sick time, vacation time and health insurance change, if at all?
- If there is a plan to increase gross margins, how will this actually happen?
- Are there any overlapping products, customers, competitors?

116

We try to offload as much work as we can to resolve these issues for the business owner, but it still takes an enormous amount of time. As compared with the financial buyer deal we did, there were more trips and meetings, and more of the seller's employees were involved with the strategic deal.

In contrast to a financial buyer, who can be thought of as a partner that can lend financial and management assistance, the strategic buyer provided our client a home – an organization that has vast resources and complementary products and services.

The Financial Buyer

Our other client provided economic modeling products and services to a wide variety of customers. They collect and analyze labor and economic data, and, although they use very sophisticated modeling, they output plain language results. For example, if you are an employer, you can choose a geographic area and do a what-if analysis by simulating moving a facility with 50 jobs to that area. The model may tell you that you will actually add 83 total jobs because of the net impact of creating those core jobs.

We brought our client to market and were able to bring 10 offer letters to the owners of the company. Meetings and negotiations followed, and a private equity group from Palo Alto came out on top. Purchase price in terms of cash, equity, notes and earn-out is, of course, part of the equation, but this PE group was also chosen because of the value they could add to the company and the personal connection they built with the owners.

A financial partner was important to our client because the owners will continue to run the company and are not ready to completely cash out yet. So retaining equity was important for that proverbial "second bite of the apple." Plus, the owners made it clear they were enjoying the ride and were looking forward to working with a financial partner to grow the company (but not on their nickel any longer).

The chosen PE group is a quality private equity group run by three bright young guys. JR, the principle, has owned, operated and sold a business before. He is the front man and was our main contact throughout the transaction. One guy ran the financial models (and re-ran the models, and re-ran the models) and watched out for their financial interest, while the third guy was the technical guru. He did the technical due diligence on our client and will be key in helping them as the company grows.

In comparison to a strategic buyer, a financial buyer tends to focus on the financials and, specifically, the earnings. After all, that is exactly what they are paying for. You can be sure that, at the end of due diligence, there was no question in anyone's mind what the earnings actually were. A third party financial due diligence consultant was hired who came in and scrubbed the numbers. I was extremely nervous about that because I thought that firm might try to justify its expense by making sure it found something to subtract from earnings. They did, but they also found some things that added to earnings.

Although focused on the numbers, the PE group was able to step back and take a more holistic view when required, and I really appreciated that. After all, it is not in any buyer's or seller's interest to create a rocky relationship by arguing over a few dollars.

In contrast to a strategic buyer, who will usually buy 100 percent, our client found a partner who can help finance growth and provide management assistance. It is a good match, and there is no question in my mind that they will be a larger, more professional company in a short amount of time.

Deal structuring and getting what you want

When we first meet business owners wishing to sell, many have a pre-conceived notion of what a sale may look like. They may believe they have to sell 100 percent of the company, or that they will be forced to stay, made to leave, etc. These two middle-market deals we closed illustrate how deals can be structured to give owners what they want.

Company 1: Partial Buyout, Recapitalization, Equity Rollover

With one of the recent middle-market deals, there were three owners. Two were founders who built the company based on their excellent reputation within the industry. The third owner, who was much younger than the founders, joined the company later and became CEO. He was able to grow the company in the later stages using web and internet technologies. Although the two founders were starting to think about retirement, the CEO wanted to stay in his role and drive the company to a new level.

A private equity buyer was ideal in this case, because it allows the young CEO to continue, albeit with professional help and guidance. The deal was structured so that the CEO was able to use some of his proceeds to "buy back" stock in the company. (Since this was an asset sale, there is a new company formed – so indeed the CEO is actually buying stock in the new company). This is typically called an equity rollover or a majority recapitalization.

Of course, an important aspect of this equity rollover is figuring out at what terms the CEO could buy stock in the new company. In this case, the CEO bought stock at the same price as the PEG – a very fair deal. In addition, there was some debt used in this deal, so the CEO was able to leverage his purchase along with the private equity group. The CEO and PEG were not completely on equal footing, as the PEG had some preferences and benefits as defined in the purchase agreement. For example, if things go badly, the PEG will usually be allowed to get their money back before the CEO will.

The two founders, looking down the road toward retirement, were not as excited about rolling their money back into the company, understandably. They decided to buy back a little bit of stock, but most of their proceeds went into retirement accounts. They also negotiated nice consulting agreements that give them flexibility to slowly wind down their involvement. In summary, the three owners got a deal that fit where they were in life and what risks they wished to take at that stage.

Company 2: 100 percent Buyout by a Strategic Acquirer

The second firm was a 100 percent buyout by a multi-billion dollar public company. Large companies generally don't buy a portion of a small company, so a partial buyout was not an option. If the seller were leaving, there would be a short transition and then they would be gone. In our case, the sellers were staying, at least for a number of years, so there was a challenge of structuring something that keeps the owners interested and engaged.

Fortunately, many strategic buyers realize the importance of having a willing and engaged business owner post-transaction. They know putting them on the payroll and giving them two weeks of vacation allowance probably isn't going to motivate an entrepreneur who has built, grown and operated their own company.

In this case the buyer used a blend of stay-on bonuses (extra pay that is really part of the purchase price), earn-out, and corporate stock options that would allow the owners to earn stock in the parent company over time. Much of the negotiations were centered on making sure the earn-outs and bonuses could be fairly earned, and not unreasonably withheld.

Even at that, some ex-business owners don't last long under new ownership. It can be too much of a change to go from running a company to having to report to a higher authority. Earn-outs help, since the opportunity to make a big upside return tends to hold someone's attention.

In my experience, many strategic buyers (and PEGs) will really bend over backwards to accommodate business owners, especially if the company is performing. If the company doesn't perform, they are not so flexible. For example, when I sold my tech company in 1997 to a public company, they wanted me to work at their headquarters in San Jose. I refused to move. Instead, I learned to fly, bought a plane and commuted for two years by plane from the foothills, across the central valley and into San Jose International Airport. It sounded ideal, but in reality as a new pilot I couldn't fly through clouds, and San Jose often has a low cloud layer in the mornings. I tried as best I could, but sometimes I had to land short at some outlying airport and wait for the fog to lift, and I did miss a few meetings. Basically, they put up with me because they needed me during the transition.

Deal attorneys

In the two deals, one seller used an experienced deal attorney while the other attempted, for a while, to use their general business attorney. Let me reiterate that you should use an attorney for the sale or purchase of your business, large or small.

The Deal Attorney

An attorney with deal experience (ask if they personally have done any transactions in the past year) is easier to work with since there are many deal terms that are common in the industry, but will be unfamiliar to a general attorney.

One of our deals used an experienced deal attorney from the start. The attorney interviewed our client and reviewed the deal terms, and was able to quickly focus on the areas of the transaction that represented some risk to our client. When the purchase agreement was delivered by the buyer, he was able to review various sections of the agreement and say, "Oh – that is standard in practically every deal and it's unlikely we will be able to change it, so let's not worry about that. This, on the other hand, I don't see in many deals and it doesn't seem reasonable."

The Other Attorney

On our other deal, the attorney, however good he was in his area of expertise, didn't have enough experience in business sales transactions to recognize – and prioritize – the most important issues. He started to go down some paths that turned out not to be relevant to the most pressing legal issues.

Soon it became apparent that an attorney with more deal experience was necessary, and we were able to recommend someone. It was an important move, as the transaction became more complex than we ever imagined because of tax issues. The first attorney would be the first to admit that he wasn't going to be able to structure the deal that we ended up with, which saved the seller in tax dollars.

The Transaction Team

It is important to note that your attorney should be thought of as a team member, not the only one driving the process. Other members of your team are your deal advisor (I stay very involved right down to the close) and your tax advisor. Sometimes an aggressive attorney can hijack the process, and that can cost both time and money. Remember – the attorney works for you. Try to keep an overall view of the transaction and your goals.

Life as an M & A advisor and Deal-Maker

I've written a blog for quite a few years. Often readers will ask what an M & A advisor is and how they can become one, so I've included some stories not so much about the art of the deal, but of being an M & A advisor.

Landing engagements and selling your services

Business owners typically contact an intermediary with many questions. The biggest one is "What is my business worth?" So, there is a dance of sorts almost right away. The business owner wants to know what you think, and you would prefer not to give an answer until you know more about the business. You don't want to set expectations too high, because it is exceedingly hard to lower them later. You also don't want to offend anyone or risk driving them away by providing a number that is too low. Unfortunately, sometimes the earnings numbers provided by business owners are not exactly the same ones that we ultimately find out the business produced.

An example of this was a business owner who actually pitched us more than we pitched him. He had heard about us and decided we were the company for him, even though he was a little shy on the minimum EBITDA we generally accept. I think we were flattered by the attention, and gave in. However, before we sign a written engagement letter we want to have a verbal agreement on what the value, or purchase price, may be. Once, when this business owner was dropping me off at the airport, I told him that we would attempt to find a strategic buyer who would pay him a premium price for his business, but that a more likely scenario would be four or five times EBITDA and we needed to agree that this price was acceptable. He switched subjects so I brought it up again, while I was standing at the car saying goodbye. He never did give me a straight answer that day and I didn't want to be rude and force the issue.

We shouldn't have taken the engagement without further clarity on expected value. Furthermore, when we did the full analysis on earnings, they were quite a bit lower than the business owner had thought they were. It was a simple mistake of having his CPA make adjustments, and then having the business owner make them again, so he was double adjusting for depreciation, interest, etc.

We went ahead with our marketing, and we did get offers – including a good, straightforward offer at five times earnings. Unfortunately, the owner's expectations were much higher, and he rejected the offer. That was a year of hard work wasted. However, I knew it was partially my fault for not making sure we had explicit agreement on value from the start.

Meeting with business owners

This is the best part of the job – going out to meet with business owners and discovering the inner workings of the company. During these visits I learn what the company history is, where the business is now and – most importantly for selling a business – what the growth opportunities are.

Photo 1, Stop at roadhouse airstrip in Oregon

I do deals over a large territory in the Western United States. You could say it is fortunate that I'm a pilot with my own airplane, but I think I probably cover such a large area because I enjoy flying so much. I also thoroughly enjoy meeting different people and visiting businesses in some of the more rural areas of our country. For example, I once took a trip north to visit a prospective client in the Pullman, Wash./Moscow, Idaho area, and then on to visit another prospect near Seattle. I'm continually surprised how large and expansive our country is. I flew for over three hours on this trip and flew over only one small city (Baker City, Ore.). The rest was high desert, mountains, lakes, and farmland.

The company I visited on the first part of this particular trip is in a relatively remote area, but one that is well known because of the local universities. Pullman is the home of Washington State University, while Moscow is the home of University of Idaho. The company is able to attract educated, highly capable and extremely loyal employees, and for less than one would have to pay in a large city.

At first, I was worried that the business was too dependent on the founder. That's a common problem with any mid-sized company, especially one with as a complex set of products and services as this one. Fortunately, the founder anticipated this, and has been working for the last four years to create a management and technology layer that would

Photo 2, Mt. Hood, OR

supplant him, and allow him to work on projects that help position the company in the future as a worldwide player. We later engaged this company as our client.

I then flew west past Seattle and landed on an island in Puget Sound, in the rain, of course. This company had a major challenge – one customer accounted for 95 percent of its business. Since most private equity groups will worry if customer concentration is above 15 or 20 percent, 95 percent is really a challenge. Fortunately, the one customer was Home Depot, so the real challenge was finding a strategic acquirer that valued the relationship with Home Depot.

My meeting with the company was mainly about strategizing and estimating value based on their Home Depot relationship. I had to explain that we would market to the many thousands of private equity groups and relevant strategic acquirers, but, in this case, the vast majority would drop out immediately. We later landed this engagement.

Buyer/seller meetings: Smoke jumping

I represented a company that rented emergency communications equipment to the U.S. government, primarily temporary air traffic control towers for helicopter fire-fighting operations. This company had a lot of interest from prospective buyers, and I ended up with two serious candidates – one an individual and one a private equity group. That summer, some large fires burned for several months in eastern Washington, providing an excellent opportunity for these buyers to see the company in action.

Photo 3, Washington Fire

I enjoy working with interesting companies, and I also enjoy flying out to meet with clients or host management meetings with buyers and sellers.

However, I couldn't even begin to convince my wife this was going to be a typical trip – I was obviously excited to be able to fly into an active fire-fighting operations area for the meetings.

I flew out of my home base in the California foothills before dawn on a

Photo 4, Flying through smoke

Tuesday morning in my Cessna, and spent a nervous flight heading to Omak, Wash. to meet with my client before the first buyer showed up. Obviously, there could be a lot of smoke from the fires and I was worried about getting in safely. However, a temporary control tower had been set up to handle the fire-fighting aircraft and they brought me right in. It was smoky, but there were still probably 5 to 7 miles of visibility. My client had let the control tower personnel know I was coming and they didn't miss a beat when I read my tail number to them.

Photo 5, Mobile traffic control "tower"

Unfortunately, my client's equipment had been "demobilized" at Omak and moved over to Methow Valley. The airport there is deeper in the mountains, and they were reporting 2 to 5 miles visibility in smoke. That is too much for me. So I left my plane at Omak and the client was nice enough to drive me to Methow Valley.

We had a great meeting with the first buyer. This buyer was technically-savvy and spent time examining the equipment and talking about technical issues with the business owner. He and I spent that night camping with exhausted firefighters on the lawn of the Cascade Smokejumpers facility. We sat at dusk watching a new column of smoke rise over the hill. My client commented that he loved the color of smoke at sunset. "It's the color of money," he said.

We were able to attend the morning strategy meeting for the fire-fighting effort, which was fascinating to say the least. About half the meeting was strategy, and the other half was safety-oriented with backup plans.

129

I was supposed to fly to Spokane and pick up the next buyer the following morning, so I got a ride to my plane and, during the pre-flight inspection, discovered some oil on the ground and on the belly. There wasn't a lot, but oil on the ground is never a good sign. I spent about 20 minutes finding the leak, and found that it was in the oil line that leads to the firewall and eventually to the oil pressure gauge in the panel. That oil line is designed to hold pressure, but not leak much oil if damaged. So I was confident I could fill the oil to the top and make it to Spokane. I got a hold of a mechanic there who would meet me, and I made the 40-minute flight without incident.

I left the plane in Spokane to be repaired, and drove the next buyer into fire camp the next morning, a good three hours away. Flying is much better. We had another good meeting, this one more financially-oriented, since this buyer was from a private equity group. We drove back to Spokane the same day, and fortunately my plane was fixed and ready to go.

However, this emergency equipment rental company engagement was a great example of how you can work hard in this business, only to have a deal fall through for no fault of your own. In this case, it was an act of God. It rained.

After the visits to the fire camp, both buyers firmed up their preliminary offers for the company. The seller and I had both been upfront with the buyers about the obvious – not every year is a big fire year. However, this particular year was shaping up to be a big fire year and the blaze the buyers observed was a large, complex fire of three or four individual fires in fairly close proximity. About 10 days after the fire camp visit, it rained and simply put the fires out. That ended fire season and capped the revenue and profits of the company quite a bit lower than expected.

The offers disappeared along with the fires. Why couldn't that perfectly fine string of devastating fires continue? I'm kidding, but it is frustrating to work hard for a year on a deal and have it disappear.

Flying south

Photo 6, Near Sedona

On another occasion, my partner Graeme Plant and I went on business tour of the Southwest. We got an early start, taking off at 6 a.m. I enjoy flying over the Southwest, even though much of it seems rather barren from the air. I've learned that some of that barren terrain is quite beautiful and complex when appreciated from the ground. I've also learned much of it is truly barren, which is why I always keep two small backpacks with survival gear in the plane, should I have to unexpectedly land somewhere.

We landed in Kingman, Ariz. after a three-hour flight to visit the first business owner, who graciously picked us up at the airport. This $20 million business is one that I would expect to be affected by the economy, but the owner has worked hard to open new accounts and expand distribution. He has a lot of energy and is even working with the National Basketball Association on a distribution deal. We had a good meeting, strategizing with the owner about which sectors and countries were the best to market his company to. We later landed this company as a client.

We then flew to Scottsdale, Ariz. for our next meeting, where we met Larry Reinharz who had flown in from our corporate office in Connecticut. Scottsdale is a wealthy community, and it shows at the airport. The private air terminal had a Ferrari in the lobby, and my plane was the only aircraft with a propeller on the ramp. I know a place like this doesn't make its money on pilots like me, but they know how to run a business and treat all their customers the same. So, we were able to enjoy a free crew car to get a sandwich and then the use of their conference facilities.

The business owner we met with was successful, but, at first, I didn't believe much he was saying. He said he didn't actually do anything. Many owners say this, but it turns out they actually do quite a bit and generally work hard. He finally got us to believe that, truly, he didn't do anything. This was a first for me and I don't believe I will ever see another company like this. We later landed this company as a client, but the company fell apart after a major partnership disagreement.

Photo 7, Somewhere near Hollywood

After the meeting we flew to Carlsbad, Calif., a little north of San Diego, with Larry sitting in the co-pilot's seat. I had to be mentally alert for the flying and for the meetings, and it was just too much thinking in one day for me. So, when we arrived, I went to bed while Larry and Graeme went out for dinner.

The meeting the next morning was with the owner of an electronics company. We all decided (including the owner) that we needed to wait a bit and see how he continued to perform in this economy. Sometimes the best route is to wait it out and sell when the trend is flat or up. We later tried to land this engagement, but the owner refused to pay an up-front fee, and we parted ways.

We had one final meeting near Burbank, Calif., so we took off from Carlsbad and headed straight over L.A. I was a little nervous, because this was difficult flying for me. I filed an instrument flight plan, which means you have to carefully follow the plan and the invariable mid-flight changes they give to you. The radio traffic is incessant and there isn't much time between waypoints to figure things out. At one point, we were flying right next to LAX, which was both fun and nerve-wracking. I did fine, and soon we were making a right turn for a long final approach into Burbank airport.

Photo 8, Sunset

We rented a car and drove to a neighboring city for the last meeting. I was impressed with some of the companies we meet during the trip, but this company seemed to have it all. It was a solid, technical company with a highly credentialed staff and a reputation that has provided them with an impressive backlog. The owner was a bright, articulate professional whom we were sure would impress any buyer. We eventually landed this company as a client.

After the meeting we said goodbye to Larry, and we took off out of Burbank in time to get home to Northern California at a decent hour. All in all, a very productive trip.

Exciting times: Meeting walkouts

We had a client who was an absolute expert in his field. However, out of his area of expertise he was rather naïve and that really came to hurt us while selling the company. We found a strategic buyer – a $6 billion dollar public company well-known for paying a healthy price to purchase businesses. Two guys from this company got the book and financials, called back with a few questions, and then arranged to travel from the east coast to meet the sellers at their place in California. I rented a conference room in a nearby hotel and asked the buyers to get there 30 minutes early so I could brief them on what to expect. I should have given them much more time before the real meeting started.

The meeting with the buyer and seller hadn't gone on for all but 30 minutes and I could tell the seller, my client, was getting agitated. He demanded to know how a certain division of this public company could help his company grow. The buyers responded that they were not actually from that division and couldn't answer the question, but they did answer from their perspective. It seemed perfectly reasonable to me because, after all, this was a company with no less than 30 divisions, so not everyone is going to know everything.

The seller, with obvious disdain for the answer, got up and left. I was dumbfounded. The buyers suggested that perhaps they should head back to the airport. I asked them to hold on, and that I would go talk to the seller. I found him under an umbrella out on a patio. He said, at first, he worried that they were only trying to gather information to compete with him. Then, he was angry when he realized that they knew very little about his operation. He felt they should have done more research before coming out. I tried to tell him that they had traveled all the way out to see him, and it was rude to walk out on them.

He dismissed that outright, and said, "It doesn't matter. People do this all the time during negotiations." I told him this wasn't a negotiation – it was supposed to be a friendly meeting to get to know each other. I convinced him to come back and be nice, but the rest of the meeting was awkward. The buyer called the next morning and passed on the opportunity. I'm surprised they didn't do it right after the meeting.

The most amazing thing was that the seller said later that this company would be a good buyer! I think he could sense my jaw dropping, and went on to add that, though the company was fine, the two guys they sent were worthless. I had to tell him that we could probably assume this company was no longer interested.

Mundane tasks – Doing what it takes

Flying into fire camp is great, but the business isn't always as exciting as that. I've had two memorable days scanning documents, and not memorable in the positive sense.

Photo 9, Stacks of contracts to scan

The first was a health-related company and the owner himself was not in good health. He ran the company mainly from his house, so many of the contracts and documents that the buyer wanted to see during due diligence were kept in file cabinets at the owner's home. My partner and I offered to come to his home and manually scan documents. We ended up doing more looking than scanning. His company had one large master contract with the State of California, and many small contracts derived from that master. We never could find the master contract and didn't find all the smaller contracts either. That resulted in a tough conversation with the buyer in which we had to reveal that we didn't actually have a copy of the one contract the entire business was based on.

The other memorable scanning day involved a company that had a lot of open contracts at any given time. The buyer's attorney demanded copies of all open contracts and our client's assistant just wasn't going to be able to handle the task of scanning everything. My partner Graeme and I offered to travel to their office to help, but we didn't realize the number of documents involved until we got there. We had two scanners going, and my goal for the day was to keep feeding the scanner as many pages as possible. We finished by the end of the day, which was great because I had visions of spending the weekend scanning and that didn't sound like fun.

Negotiations
A Fine Sunday Afternoon

Typically, this is not a weekend job as most buyers and sellers prefer not to spend their weekends at work. However, there are a few times when weekends and late nights are common. I remember doing final negotiations on one deal while sitting on a large rock in the Sierra Nevada mountains on a Sunday afternoon hike with my wife. Luckily, she understood and I had good phone reception.

We were down to two buyers, and they had similar offers. Both were nearing the limit of how much they would stretch and it all came down to a flurry of small cash and earn-out maneuvers. It was tough on the seller because he liked both buyers and the offers were similar, but he finally made his decision that afternoon. We finalized the letter of intent with the buyer the next morning and a deal was struck. We entered due diligence and around 60 days later closed the deal.

Greed

There is often a lot of money up for grabs in an M & A deal. As good capitalists, we will all do a little grabbing, and I find it interesting to witness the struggle with greed that many endure as a deal progresses. Some swear allegiance to their employees and talk of the bonuses these employees will receive. However, as the closing nears, that talk gets quieter and eventually dies away. Others talk little, but end up delivering in a big way to key employees.

Some inherently know what their responsibilities are after the sale. (Unfortunately, you can't completely walk away after selling a business – there are often tax, environmental and other liabilities that stay with you for a while.) Others try to slide as much responsibility as they can to the other side of the table. Although that may not be viewed as honorable, it is ethical as long as the conversation is open and transparent. However, a couple of business owners I have dealt with have gone too far by not disclosing a potential liability, and that has caused problems and ill will.

I know it is obvious, but the worst time to try to settle company ownership issues is when there is an offer on the table and money up for grabs. Given a choice between being fair and reasonable and walking away with $100,000, many will choose the money. This is why, when I take an engagement, I'll explore the ownership structure and try to ferret out any potential problems. If there are issues, I'll recommend they get an attorney involved and resolve, or at least properly document, the ownership of the business.

After years of experiencing these types of situations, I'm rarely surprised at how some people behave when there is a large amount of money involved. Maybe I'm jaded, but my opinion is that you can't positively say what you would do until you are in the situation of being able to make a grab at a large pot of money.

Probably the worst behavior I've seen was with a client who talked a lot of integrity, honesty and God. However, when we got into negotiations, he continually tried to quietly slide his liabilities onto the buyer. For example, he had an additional tax bill coming up in a year or two. At first, he wanted to keep it quiet and then was constantly trying to get that onto the buyer's plate. The simple fact was that this would be a tax on the earnings that he got before the close, and was strictly his liability. We closed the deal. But afterward, the buyer reported some environmental problems that had been hidden by seller, along with festering employee issues and quite a few safety violations.

Closing the deal

A Successful Sale is a Beautiful Thing

I once sold a private fire-fighting company that essentially rented out fire engines — complete with fire crews – primarily to the government. The company was bought by a gentleman who has two firefighters for sons. I'll call him DD for Dad of the Decade because Dad of the Year doesn't seem good enough.

There seems to always be a major challenge in selling a business. For this one, it was that the original company had a major contract to perform off-season brush clearing using prescribed burns. The company was very profitable, and we priced the business accordingly. Although the off-season contract didn't go away, it was scaled back substantially, and the previous owners refused to believe the value of their business could be reduced because of that.

It was a long and tough road for DD (and me, as the one in the middle between buyer and seller) in negotiating for the company, but he persevered and bought the company. The equipment was old and the company had some staffing problems – some of which he knew, and some of which were surprises. For example, right after taking possession of the business, he found out that all the hand-held radios were to become obsolete within a year.

DD and his sons stepped right in and worked hard. They cleaned up the facilities, repaired equipment, bought new equipment and even purchased new clothing for the crews. They instituted new rules about conduct in government fire camps. Within a year, they started building a stellar reputation. DD and his sons worked hard for off-season contracts and programs that would allow them to employ many of their core fire fighters year around. It is working.

It is tempting to celebrate the sale of a business right away, but I've learned to wait a bit. In fact, sometimes I hold my breath, hoping the buyer can run the company like it seemed like they could, and that the company itself was all it was supposed to be. In this case, things worked out well. The buyer is successful, while the sellers got a good price, and are happy and traveling in retirement.

Appendix

The following are the LOIs (letters of intent) from the "Tale of Two Deals" case study, modified to protect the identities of the companies involved. Following that is the due diligence request list from the case study. This appendix also includes a compendium of "101 Things you Should Know..." written by Ney Grant and Graeme Plant.

Tale of Two Deals: The Private Equity Letter of Intent

AMERICAN CAPITAL LLC

567 University Ave., Suite 250

Chicago, IL

PRIVATE AND CONFIDENTIAL

Gentlemen:

This letter of intent ("LOI") outlines the terms and conditions by which American Capital Co., a Utah company ("American" or the "Buyer") through a company to be formed by American ("NewCo"), proposes to complete an acquisition (the "Acquisition") of substantially all the outstanding assets of Selling Company, Inc. (the "Company") from the owners of the Company (collectively, the "Sellers"). The proposal expressed in this letter is intended to be the subject of further negotiation and then incorporated into a legally binding purchase agreement (the "Definitive Agreement," and collectively with all related documents, "Definitive Documents"), which will contain additional terms and conditions to be mutually agreed upon. Our proposal is as follows:

1.   Total Transaction Value

Subject to the contingencies contained herein, American is prepared to purchase 100 percent of the Company's assets for $7,750,000 (the "Purchase Price"), representing a multiple of 5.2 times estimated adjusted 2010 EBITDA of $1.5 million.

In exchange for the Purchase Price, American shall acquire: (i) all of the assets of the Business including all accounts receivable, prepaid assets, and other current assets; customer and vendor contracts, licenses and registrations; intellectual property, including, but not limited to, current and pending patents and trademarks, software and hardware; but excluding cash and the Company's ownership interest in real estate, if any. In addition, American is prepared to assume certain current liabilities ("Assumed Current Liabilities") of the Company, excluding retirement and profit-sharing liabilities, and otherwise as mutually agreed upon and detailed in the Definitive Agreement. No debts or other liabilities (contingent, absolute or otherwise) of the Company or any of its affiliates (other than those liabilities included in agreed upon current liabilities) or any third persons in connection with the Acquisition shall be assumed.

The $7,750,000 shall be payable with $5,750,000 in cash at closing and a $2,000,000 Seller Note as detailed below.

Buyer and Seller shall negotiate in good faith the net working capital requirements of the Company to ensure that the Company has adequate working capital including a minimum cash level of $100,000 ("Target Working Capital") at closing to conduct business in the normal course. The Purchase Price will be adjusted, on a dollar for dollar basis, if the Company's estimated net working capital (defined as non-cash current assets less Assumed Current Liabilities) differs from Target Working

Capital. As soon as practical following closing, a final closing working capital schedule shall be prepared in accordance with rules established in the Definitive Documents. Depending on the balances of the final working capital schedule, the cash purchase price may be adjusted post-closing.

2.   Sources of Capital

The financing for the cash portion of the proposed transaction shall include $3,298,400 of equity capital, $2,000,000 of which shall be provided by American, with the remaining $1,298,400 million to be provided by the Sellers. This equity capital shall take the form of Participating Preferred Stock with a 1.0 time liquidation preference and a 7 percent non-cash accumulating dividend. American's Participating Preferred Stock shall be senior in liquidation preference, including accrued dividends, to other outstanding Participating Preferred Stock.

Additional sources of capital shall include $2,250,000 million of Senior Secured Subordinated Notes (the "Notes"). The Notes shall bear 12 percent monthly cash interest, and shall be interest only for five years, and thereafter amortize in eight equal quarterly payments. The Notes shall be secured by a first lien against all of the Company's assets (other than those assets encumbered by any senior debt, in which case the Notes will have a second lien). The notes shall include detachable warrants with a nominal strike price convertible into 18 percent of NewCo on a fully-diluted basis.

$2,000,000 of Seller Notes shall be provided by the Sellers, on a pro rata basis relative to their current ownership position. The Seller Notes shall bear interest at 7 percent per annum with quarterly interest payments, with interest only through 2011 and thereafter amortizing in 16 equal quarterly payments. The Seller Notes shall be subordinated in rights of payment and upon liquidation to the Notes and any other secured debt.

Finally, American shall secure a Senior Revolving Debt facility, a portion of which shall be drawn at close.

Exhibit A, "Post-Close Capitalization and Sources & Uses of Funds" outlines the parties' expectations under this LOI.

3.   Continued Relationships

a. It is the Buyer's intention to operate the Company as a going concern. Therefore, it is our intent that essentially all current employees of the Company be retained by NewCo;

b. CEO will remain actively involved with the business for a minimum of three years, including his assumption of a position on the board of NewCo. American's interest in the Company is highly predicated and motivated by CEO's continued active involvement as Chief Executive Officer and active ongoing equity investment in the post-close company;

c. A stock option pool will be created to provide equity-based incentives to key employees, consultants, directors, and other related parties. The option pool at close will represent 12.5 percent of fully-diluted equity (with a strike price equal to the price paid by American), with 7.5 percent reserved for CEO and the remaining 5 percent for other members of the Company's ongoing management team;

d. A Shareholders' Agreement will be negotiated and executed concurrent with the closing which will, among other matters, reflect the Board make-up with American with a majority of seats and Company governance.

4.   Certain Conditions to Closing

The consummation of the proposed transaction is subject to, among other things, the satisfaction of the following conditions:

a. Execution of the Definitive Documentation, including the Definitive Agreement, and other customary documentation, satisfactory to Seller and Buyer in their sole discretion, including without limitation customary representations, warranties, and conditions to closing, including a material adverse change condition;

b. Completion by American of legal, accounting, business and environmental due diligence, with results satisfactory to American;

c. Receipt of necessary approvals or waivers by all local, state and federal regulatory bodies (including Hart Scott Rodino);

d. Receipt of all material consents, waivers or approvals of third parties necessary to consummate the transactions contemplated hereby;

e. All contractual third party consents, approvals and waivers required to consummate the transaction contemplated herein shall be obtained;

f. Execution of employment agreement(s) with existing management that is/are satisfactory to Buyer;

Execution of a Management Services agreement with American which provides for a $150,000 annual management fee paid to American. This management fee shall be paid in monthly in arrears at the rate of $12,500 per month as an ordinary business expense;

h. The Buyer shall have obtained a Senior Revolving Debt facility for the acquisition upon such terms as shall be satisfactory to Buyer.

5.   Fees and Expenses

a. Seller shall pay its legal fees, accounting fees, brokerage fees and any other fees or costs payable in conjunction with the acquisition and incurred as other than a normal part of the Company's operations. In addition, a Quality of Earnings Review (accounting due diligence) by an independent third party arranged by American shall be paid for by the Company in the event that the Transaction does not close, but otherwise by NewCo;

b. Buyer and Seller acknowledge that a broker is involved in the transaction and that the broker's fees shall be paid by Seller;

c. Upon execution of this LOI, Buyer is prepared to dedicate significant resources to consummate the Transaction in as expeditious a manner as possible. If the Transaction contemplated herein is consummated, NewCo shall reimburse Buyer upon written request for all of its fees, costs and expenses (including, without limitation, all fees, costs and expenses of its representatives) arising in connection with this Transaction.

6.   Closing Date

The closing Date shall be as soon as practical or as the parties may agree, and the parties intend to use good faith effort to close the transaction by December 31, 2010.

7.   Definitive Agreement

The Buyer and Seller shall proceed with the further negotiation, preparation and execution of Definitive Documents addressing, among other things, the points set forth in this LOI. The Definitive Agreement shall contain such joint and several representations, warranties, covenants and indemnities similar to those contained in like transactions, and as are mutually agreed upon by the parties.

8.   Due Diligence

Following the date of execution hereof, the Seller shall afford to Buyer free and full access of its offices, properties, books and records on reasonable notice during normal business hours in order to permit Buyer to make such investigation of the business, properties and operations of the Seller as it may deem necessary or desirable. The foregoing shall be subject to reasonable and appropriate procedures agreed upon among all the parties hereto. Following procedures mutually agreed to, the Seller shall allow Buyer access to its suppliers and vendors and to its customers for the purpose of assessing business relationships. American shall receive approval of CEO prior to having any discussions with customers, vendors or employees of the Company. American shall keep CEO reasonably apprised of the progress of its due diligence investigation.

9.   Confidentiality

Concurrent with the execution of this LOI, the Company agrees to keep the existence of this LOI and the terms herein strictly confidential and agrees that it will not disclose any such information to any third party (other than to X and to counsel to the Company) without the prior written consent of American.

10.   No Shopping

The Seller represents and warrants that neither they nor the Company have entered into an agreement with any other party with respect to the sale or other disposition of the assets and liabilities of the Company whether by sale, merger or other combination. The Seller agrees that prior to the earlier of (a) the termination of this LOI by three business day's advance notification from the Buyer to the Seller, (b) December 31, 2009, the Seller shall not, and shall cause Company's employees, officers, directors, shareholders, partners, affiliates, associates, advisors, agents and representatives not to, directly or indirectly, solicit, discuss or negotiate with, provide any information to, or consider the merits of any proposals or inquires from, any individual group, joint venture, partnership, corporation, association, cooperative, trust, estate or other entity of any nature (other than Buyer and its affiliates) relating to any transaction involving the sale of the business or assets of the Company or of any capital stock of the Company or any merger, consolidation or similar transaction involving the Company.

11.   Publicity

Except as required by law, the parties will agree that there will be no public announcements or other publicity with respect to the proposed transaction, this proposal, the Definitive Documents or any other matters related thereto without the express written consent of the Buyer and the Seller.

12.   Intent Only

This letter is intended merely to be a guide in the preparation of Definitive Documents satisfactory to the parties hereto. While the parties presently intend to proceed promptly to complete the Definitive Documents, it is expressly understood that this is only a letter of intent and that no liability or obligation of any nature whatsoever is intended to be created between any of the parties hereto, except with respect to the provisions of paragraphs 5, 8, 9, 10 and 11, which are binding.

13.   Expiration

This letter of intent shall expire at 5 p.m. Thursday, October 29, 2010 if not executed by both parties prior to such time.

*   *   *   *

If you agree with the foregoing terms and conditions set forth in this LOI, please execute the enclosed copies of this letter in the space provided below for your signature and return one fully executed copy to the undersigned, where upon this letter shall become a binding agreement (with respect to paragraphs 5, 8, 9, 10 and 11) upon the parties hereto and their respective heirs, successors, and assigns as to the date hereof. This LOI may be executed in several counterparts each which shall be deemed an original, but all of which counterparts collectively shall constitute one instrument.

We are excited about the prospect of working with Company management and look forward to collectively implementing the transaction and achieving accelerated, profitable growth going forward.

Accepted:

American Capital, LLC.

John Smith

Tale of Two Deals: Strategic Buyer Letter of Intent
AMERICAN REALLY BIG PUBLIC COMPANY

CONFIDENTIAL

Dear Seller,

We are very impressed by what Company has achieved independently in establishing a strong market position backed by an excellent range of products. While in other cases we would only be beginning to get to know a company at this stage in the process, the successful, long-term business relationship between American and the Company gives us great confidence that both companies will benefit from even greater alignment. Consequently, we are pleased to express American, Inc.'s ("American") interest in acquiring Company, Inc. ("Company" or "the Company").

We feel strongly that the benefits of this proposed transaction would benefit both companies in many ways. For example, a transaction would provide opportunity for greater collaboration on technology development, building on what we started with YTQ. Also, we believe that a transaction would enable us to better align our sales and marketing activities to help customers understand the benefits that we can jointly bring.

With this experience, combined with our familiarity with Company's markets, we believe we can complete a transaction efficiently. We will provide an information request list within two business days following the receipt of this letter countersigned by the Company. We would schedule on-site due diligence to commence about one week following the submission of our request list and we anticipate the on-site due diligence to last several days. Further, we would provide to you a draft of the purchase agreement within two weeks following the completion of our on-site due diligence. We feel comfortable that, assuming your cooperation, we could sign a definitive agreement approximately six weeks after entering into this letter of intent providing us exclusivity.

Our non-binding offer for Company on a cash-free, debt-free basis is $14.5 million in cash based on the financial information provided in the confidential descriptive memorandum. We would intend to pay the purchase price from cash on hand. Out of this purchase price, $1 million would be paid in retention consideration on the second anniversary and $2.5 million would be paid in deferred consideration. The precise terms for the deferred consideration would be mutually agreed upon during the next phase of the transaction process.

Larry, consistent with your conversations with Jim, we understand that your compensation has approximated $240,000 annually. We would expect that, consistent with other executives, your compensation package would shift to some of your compensation being tied to incentive compensation.

Furthermore, during the next phase of the process, we would like to discuss with you the future growth of the business so that we have a better understanding of its long-term facility requirements. We would work with you to come up with a mutually agreeable lease term at a fair market value lease rate for the facility.

Since we are looking forward to working with the Company team to continue building the business, we would want to structure with you an appropriate retention plan for key employees. Our intent is to provide strong incentives for key employees to remain with the Company after the transaction, and we look forward to discussing with you how best to achieve this goal. Our proposal assumes the shareholders, management and key personnel would similarly be committed to a successful transaction in the long-term and would sign non-compete agreements in conjunction with the transaction.

This non-binding proposal is contingent on confirmatory business and legal due diligence results satisfactory to American Board approval, any necessary regulatory approvals and mutually acceptable acquisition documentation that will contain customary representations, warranties and indemnification provisions, including an indemnification holdback, from the Company and shareholders of the Company.

By countersigning this letter below, you agree that in consideration of and to facilitate our mutual discussions regarding the potential transaction with American, the Company and its affiliates, agents and shareholders will grant us exclusive dealing in our potential transaction. As such, none of the Company, its affiliates, agents or shareholders will discuss or negotiate with, or accept an offer from, any other party with respect to the purchase of, or investment in, the Company, including the acquisition of any material assets of the Company, during a period extending initially from the date a copy of this letter countersigned by the Company is received by American until 6 p.m. (New York City time) on the 45th day thereafter (it being understood that the Company shall be free to simply advise third parties that it is prohibited from holding discussions or negotiations concerning the Company or a transaction). Unless written notice of termination is delivered by either the Company or American to the other at least five business days prior to the end of the exclusivity period, the period of exclusivity will be extended indefinitely until five business days after delivery of a written notice of termination by either party to the other. The existence and terms and conditions of this letter are strictly confidential and may not be disclosed by the Company, its affiliates, agents or shareholders to anyone other than to the directors, officers and advisors of the Company who have fiduciary or legal responsibilities to the Company to keep such information confidential.

Unless and until a definitive agreement regarding a potential transaction is negotiated and executed between the parties, neither party shall be obligated with respect to any transaction and no obligation or rights or liabilities of any kind whatsoever are created (or shall be deemed to be created) as a result of this letter, or any other written or oral statement or any further actions by the parties, except in the case of this letter for the provisions contained in the preceding paragraph and this paragraph. Accordingly, subject to your obligations under the aforementioned exclusivity provisions, either party is free to abandon discussions regarding the potential transaction at any time for any reason or for no reason and the decision of either party to so abandon discussions shall not be subject to legal challenge by the other. Neither this paragraph nor the preceding paragraph of this letter can be waived or amended except by the written consent of both parties; and, no other paragraph of this letter can be waived or amended without our prior written consent. For purposes of this paragraph, the term "definitive agreement" does not include this letter, an executed letter of intent or any other preliminary written agreement nor does it include any written or verbal acceptance of an offer or bid. This letter, and all claims or causes of action that may be based upon, arise out of or relate to this letter or the negotiation, execution or performance hereof, shall be governed by the internal laws of the State of New York.

We are excited about the prospects of American acquiring Company. Please call me at 555-1234 if you need further clarification of our offer. We look forward to hearing from you.

Sincerely,

AMERICAN COMPANY, INC.

Tale of Two Deals: Due Diligence Request List

The following is a due diligence request list used in one of the "Two Deal" deals. It was provided by the buyer's counsel. Often this list is loaded into an electronic deal room and everything is done electronically. In this case, it was done the old fashion way by creating binders with tabbed sections.

(The "Company")	
Due Diligence Request List	
#	Item
1	**Real and Personal Property**
a.	Descriptions of all real property owned by the Company, including title insurance policies, legal descriptions, maps and title abstracts.
b.	All contracts or options to purchase real property to which the

	Company is a party.
c.	All real property leases to which the Company is party, including any subleases, assignments, estoppel letters, non-disturbance agreements, guarantees, deposits or letters of credit relating to such leases.
d.	All certificates of occupancy, zoning variances and local permits and estoppel letters and related applications therefore.
e.	Descriptions of all real property formerly owned, leased or operated by the Company and a list of all jurisdictions where the Company has conducted business.
f.	All personal property leases to which the Company is party, including any assignments or guarantees relating to such leases.
g.	A list of equipment and machinery owned or leased by the Company (indicating whether such equipment and machinery is owned or leased).
h.	Copies of any construction agreements for construction or alteration of any real property of the Company.
i.	Copies of all correspondence or documentation relating to inspection reports on the physical condition of the Company's real property.
2	**Intellectual Property**
a.	Patents.
(i)	A schedule of patents and patent applications used by the Company, identified by country, patent number, issue date, expiration date, applicant(s), title, status (including maintenance fees status, file history and whether being worked in nations so requiring, and current owner).
(ii)	A schedule of each invention disclosure for which patent applications may be contemplated but have not been filed,

	showing subject matter, inventor, date of first use, sale or disclosure, and status.
(iii)	All un-issued and issued U.S. patents and patent applications and their respective file histories.
(iv)	All files and information on patent reissues or re-examinations, whether pending or complete.
(v)	Any interference history of files pertaining to any interference for all patent or patent applications.
(vi)	Any litigation records past, ongoing, or threatened relating to any of the technology held by the Company or third party agreements.
(vii)	Any validity or infringement opinions concerning any patents prepared for the Company.
(viii)	Any legal documents (research contracts, licensing agreements, assignments, etc.) with third parties (other companies or universities) that could impact the Company's ability to commercialize products from any part of its ongoing programs.
b.	A schedule of trademark (service mark and trade dress) registrations and applications identifying each mark and including date of registration (application), registration number, status (registered, reviewed or abandoned), Section 8 and 15 affidavits submitted, etc., and each country or state where registered. In those instances where registration has not been sought, identify each mark, trade dress or trade name and its date of first use anywhere in the U.S. Identify any such mark where rights are based in intent-to-use.
c.	A schedule of copyright registrations and applications identifying each copyright by title, registration number and date of registration.

d.	All other material intellectual property rights of or used by the Company whether owned or licensed from or to any third party and any license agreement relating thereto.
e.	All manuals or other written documents detailing the Company's policies and procedures for protecting trade secrets.
f.	All licensing agreements, merchandising agreements (naming the Company as licensee or licensor) or assignments relating to patents, technology, trade secrets, trademarks (service marks), trade dress, copyrights and websites.
g.	Any communications from third parties relating to the validity or infringement of the Company's technology, trade secrets, trademarks, service marks, trade dress or copyrights.
h.	Any study or report relating to the validity or value of the Company's patents, technology, trade secrets, trademarks, service marks, trade dress or copyrights.
i.	All other documents, agreements or information relating to the Company's right to use intellectual property or any item of technology that is used or useful in the conduct of its business, including without limitation, licenses and sublicenses, option agreements, disclosure agreements, escrow agreements, technology transfer agreements, development agreements, distribution agreements and finance and security agreements, that is not described above.
j.	A complete list of all judgments, decrees and other orders of courts or agencies that restrict the Company in the use of its intellectual property rights.
k.	A complete list of all disputes or assertions (including infringement) of purported rights to which the Company is or was a party within the past seven years that involve the Company or third party intellectual property, showing the

	nature, potential exposure and status of each.
l.	Copies of agreements, policies or other arrangements relating to proprietary rights of employees in products of the Company (including royalty or other fee arrangements).
3	**Litigation**
a.	A complete list and summary of the facts of all third party litigation, suits and other proceedings or investigations, including governmental or regulatory proceedings or investigations.
b.	A complete list and summary of the facts surrounding any pending or threatened proceedings or investigations involving the Company. Please include estimates of the potential exposure and a narrative discussion of the status of each.
c.	A summary of any investigations or inquiries regarding regulatory compliance (FTC, FDA, OSHA, EPA, EEOC, etc.).
d.	Description of all workers' compensations claims made in the past five years.
e.	A complete list and summary of the facts surrounding any labor disputes.
f.	Audit letter responses from outside counsel for the past five years.
g.	Copies of consent decrees or judgments under which there are continuing or contingent obligations.
4	**Licenses and Regulatory Compliance**
a.	All licenses, permits and registrations related to the operation of the Company's facilities, equipment and business issued by federal, state, local or foreign authorities.

b.	Evidence of compliance with, or notices of non-compliance with, alleged violations of or any deficiencies with respect to (including any liens or other limitations imposed on the real property of the Company) various acts and regulations, as applicable, including:
(i)	The Occupational Safety and Health Act and all regulations promulgated thereunder;
(ii)	The Employee Retirement Income Security Act of 1974, as amended;
(iii)	Equal Employment Opportunities Act;
(iv)	Labor practices regulation;
(v)	The Age Discrimination in Employment Act of 1967, as amended;
(vi)	Title VII of the Civil Rights Act of 1964, as amended; or
(vii)	The Americans with Disabilities Act of 1990.
c.	All filings, consents, authorizations, certificates, audit papers and other documentation or communications relating to compliance with federal, state or local statutory or regulatory requirements for the past five years.
d.	A list of trade association memberships including any agreements, permits or certifications relating thereto.
5	**Contracts and Commitments**
a.	Contracts, agreements, commitments and leases (and any and all amendments, modifications, waivers or consents relating thereto) which involve receipt or payment by the Company of more than $1,000, including, but not limited to, the following:
(i)	Agency or sales representative agreements.
(ii)	Licensing agreements.

(iii)	Operating agreements, joint venture agreements, partnership agreements, and consulting agreements.
(iv)	Government contracts.
(v)	Contracts with customers. (Include a standard form of customer contract, if applicable.)
(vi)	Any contract or agreement between the Company and any of its present or former stockholders, officers or directors or any of their affiliates.
(vii)	Any contract or agreement pertaining to the Company to which any of its stockholders, officers or directors or any of their affiliates is a party.
(viii)	All loan agreements, revolving credit agreements, financing leases, or other debt instruments. Include any notifications of any alleged breach or near breach of any material covenant relating to any of such borrowings.
(ix)	A description of any encumbrances, restrictions and claims affecting any real or personal property.
(x)	All mortgages, indentures, trust agreements, security agreements and guarantees.
(xi)	Copies of all acquisition or sale agreements and related documentation relating to the acquisition or divestiture of any material assets, entities or business operations of the Company during the past five years.
(xii)	All non-competition agreements and confidentiality agreements to which the Company or any of its stockholders, officers, directors or affiliates is a party.
(xiii)	All maintenance agreements.
(xiv)	All equipment leases and other personal property leases.
(xv)	All service agreements (including those related to market

	research, advertising or similar services).
(xvi)	All contracts or agreements of the Company or its subsidiaries to indemnify third parties for any loss.
(xvii)	All agreements to provide services at below cost (other than promotional arrangements entered into in the ordinary course of business).
(xviii)	All development agreements.
(xix)	Any other material agreements.
6	**Insurance**
	Please provide copies of all insurance policies.
7	**Taxes and Financial Information**
a.	All audit and revenue agent reports (federal, state and local) for the preceding five years.
b.	All settlement documents and any related correspondence with taxing authorities for the past three years.
c.	All agreements extending time for filing tax returns or waiving statute of limitations.
d.	Any other communication or agreement between the Company and the Internal Revenue Service, or any state or local tax authority, for the preceding five years.
e.	Powers of attorney with respect to tax matters.
f.	All tax sharing, indemnification or allocation agreements.
g.	A list of all jurisdictions (whether foreign or domestic) in which the Company is obligated to pay taxes.
h.	All auditors' letters to management and management's and counsel's letters to auditors of the Company with respect to its audits for the preceding five years.

i.	Copies of consolidated audited financial statements of the Company for the five most recent fiscal years, as well as the most recent un-audited statements, with comparable statements for the most recent fiscal year.
j.	All documents relating to the Company's S Corporation status.
8	**Employment Policies and Personnel**
a.	All contracts with employees, officers or directors, including, but not limited to:
(i)	Management and employment agreements.
(ii)	Secrecy, confidentiality, and non-competition agreements.
(iii)	Golden parachutes.
(iv)	Collective bargaining agreements.
(v)	Indemnification arrangements.
b.	Policies. Please provide the Employee handbook or manual, and a brief description of the following policies:
(i)	Severance pay.
(ii)	Moving expenses.
(iii)	Vacation and holidays.
(iv)	Tuition reimbursement.
(v)	Salary review.
(vi)	Loans (include information or agreements regarding any outstanding loans to employees).
(vii)	Advances and reimbursement of expenses.
(viii)	Disability policies.
c.	Employee benefit plans. Please provide plan documents and agreements, including trust agreements (where applicable) and most recent Form 5500 (where applicable) for each of the

	following:
(i)	Pension program or retirement benefits.
(ii)	Cash or stock profit sharing plan or bonus arrangements.
(iii)	Savings plans, including 401K.
(iv)	Insurance Plans: Health, Accident, Life, etc.
(v)	Deferred compensation.
(vi)	Death benefits.
(vii)	Individual or group bonus plans.
(viii)	Stock option or appreciation rights arrangements, ESOP and stock bonus plans and arrangements.
d.	Labor History.
(i)	All collective bargaining agreements and employee management pacts.
(ii)	List of negotiations during most recent five years with any unit or group seeking to become the bargaining unit for employees.
(iii)	List of any union representation elections currently scheduled or taking place during most recent five years.
(iv)	A summary of any work stoppages, strikes or slowdowns by employees taking place during most recent five years.
(v)	Requests for arbitration, grievance proceedings, etc. in labor disputes, including all written documentation related thereto. Also include a narrative description of all union organizing activity (such as card checks) at any of the Company's facilities.
(vi)	OSHA and workmen compensation history.
(vii)	Summaries of any age, sex, disability, national origin and race discrimination claims.

(viii)	A schedule showing head count (by division, if applicable), turnover and material absentee history of employees for the past five years.
e.	A list of all states where employees or independent contractors are located.
9	**Corporate Organization**
a.	Articles of Incorporation, Charter and Bylaws of the Company, and all amendments thereto.
b.	All corporate stock, lists of stockholders and related records.
c.	All minute books of the Company (include copies of all minutes of the meetings of the stockholders or directors for the past five years).
d.	All change of ownership agreements, stockholder agreements, and other voting agreements.
e.	A list and description of all capital stock or other equity or ownership or proprietary interest in any corporation, partnership, association, trust, joint venture or other entity owned or held by the Company.
f.	Qualifications to do business in jurisdictions in which the Company is currently operating or has operated.
g.	Current certificates of authority, good standing and tax status for all applicable jurisdictions.
h.	All ESOP, stock bonus, option, shareholder or other agreements to issue shares with respect to the Company and the aggregate number of shares subject thereto.
i.	List of all members of the Board of Directors and officers of the Company and any subsidiaries.
j.	List of all assumed fictitious names and other business or trade names under which the Company and any subsidiaries are

	conducting or have conducted business.
k.	A description of all contractual restrictions on transfer of the capital stock or assets of the Company and any subsidiaries.
10	**Miscellaneous Matters**
a.	All press releases issued by the Company during the past year.
b.	Copies of all recent articles or brochures relating to the Company or any of its products or services.
c.	All other documents viewed by the Company as material to its operations.

101 Things You Should Know About Selling Your Business

Planning and Preparation

1. Don't wake up one day and decide to sell.

   Wake up and decide to plan for the exit. Meet an advisor at least a year before selling so you know the process and perhaps can even increase the purchase price through planning.

2. High earnings equal a high selling price.

   Above all else, this is the main factor driving value.

3. Depreciate this!

   Earnings (both discretionary earnings for small companies and EBITDA for larger ones) don't include depreciation expense. For tax reasons, business owners tend to expense rather than capitalize and depreciate, but in the year or two before a sale? Depreciate.

4. Reduce working capital needs.

   A mid-size company is sold with enough working capital ("current assets minus current liabilities") to continue to operate the business. Think of it as having to sell your car with gas in the tank. Prove you can reduce this amount now and you can take more cash home in the deal later.

5. Nix the C-Corp.

If you think it will be a number of years before you close a deal, see if you can take an S-Corp election. Most buyers will want to do an asset sale and the double tax created by a C-Corp can be painful.

6. Concentration is a bad word.

Businesses with high customer concentration or supplier concentration attract fewer buyers and this lowers the price. Having a customer with 25 percent or more of your business, or having a supplier with 40 percent of your business is high. Diversify if at all possible.

7. Make yourself un-important.

What business would you rather buy? The one where the owner takes frequent trips and takes every Friday off, or one where the owner has to come in even when he is sick because the place will fall apart without him? A company that relies on the owner gets far less cash up front and more in down-the-road payments.

8. Pay some taxes.

Yes, everyone plays the tax avoidance game, but only to a degree. An advisor can only adjust earnings only so much, so it is far better to just pay your taxes for a few years before a sale than to endure any possible complications from avoiding them.

9. Understand what "adjusted earnings" means.

Now, well before a sale, is the time to understand what adjusted seller's discretionary earnings and/or EBITDA really means. For example, some expenses will be valid adjustments, so there would be no need to work on reducing that expense, while other areas may need some real focus.

10. A risky business is a cheap business.

Do you have legal issues dragging on? Environmental problem lurking? Buyers hate risks and risks tangibly lower the price. Identify and attack these areas before a sale.

11. Pick that low-hanging fruit.

    Many business owners say things like, "Pay me X, because you can simply grow this company by doing Y, but I didn't want to do that (Y) because of Z." For example, "All you have to do is hire a sales manager, but I didn't because I don't manage people well". If you have an easy way to boost sales, do it, because you are not going to get X otherwise.

12. Get a planner, if you don't already have one.

    A financial planner can tell you what you will need to net from a deal to reach your financial goals.

13. There's more to life than money.

    You've heard that no one on their death bed said, "I should have spent more time at the office." Think about your financial goals, but also take stock of the other things you want to do in life. Holding off on selling to get an extra million may mean never getting to do some things that mean a lot to you.

14. Organize.

    You will be asked to produce all the paperwork that verifies your company's standing, your contractual relationships, permits, licenses, etc. Get that ready early so you can do it on your schedule.

15. Get a legal checkup.

    If you have an attorney, ask him or her to make sure all of your legal work is current. (Like stock ownership records)

16. Get an accounting checkup.

    Meet with your accountant and make sure the books are in order.

17. Get Compiled or Reviewed financial statements.

    Most middle market companies are sold with reviewed or compiled (not audited) financial statements for the three prior year.. If you are thinking of selling in the next few years, consider going the extra step and getting these done.

18. Get ready for a six to 12-month sales process.

    The length of time to sell doesn't seem to depend much on company size. It takes six months to sell if everything goes right. It rarely does, so nine to 12 months is a more realistic number to plan for.

19. Get greedy.

    A year or two before a sale is the time to be greedy, for it is then that you can really impact value by focusing on controlling costs and boosting earnings.

Getting Ready to Go To Market

20. Don't get greedy.

    Unreasonable expectations have killed many a deal. Get good advice up front about value, then don't do the "value creep." The most frustrating thing as an advisor is to get a good offer based on what an owner said they wanted, only to find out they have since changed their mind and now want more.

21. Clean up.

    A clean site makes a better impression on potential investors than a property that's unkempt.

22. Identify your dream team.

    You need an intermediary (probably), a transaction attorney, a good CPA and, hopefully, you'll need a financial advisor to help you invest your now diversified portfolio.

23. Use a business broker

    For companies with earnings less than $500,000 use a main street broker. A broker will allow you to run the business while they work with buyers.

24. Don't use a business broker.

For companies with earnings larger than $500,000 use a high-end broker or M & A advisor. For earnings over $1 million, use an M & A advisor / investment bank.

25. Don't use anyone.

Don't use an intermediary if you are selling to a key employee, family member or have a distressed situation with a small business. Do use an attorney and a CPA.

26. Get all-star attorneys referred to you.

Your intermediary is often a good source of referrals for deal attorneys. An ongoing relationship between attorneys and intermediaries means the attorney has an incentive to keep fees down so they can get future referrals.

27. Get all-star intermediaries referred to you.

If you already have a good deal attorney, ask them about good intermediaries.

28. Call references.

Ask prospective intermediaries for references. Then call them. Often, we give people references and they don't call. I don't know why they don't call, but you really should.

29. Ask about the up front fee

Middle market M & A firms charge an upfront fee. That fee should be used to market the company, not pay large commissions to the salespeople and/or M & A advisors. Otherwise the incentive is to sign up clients, not sell companies. Just ask.

30. Answer the postcard, letter or phone call that says, "We have a buyer for your business."

I'm kidding, because they don't have buyers. But you knew that.

31. Fire your attorney.

If your attorney doesn't have experience with business sales transactions, get one that does. A generalist attorney can spin his wheels pretty hard trying to get up to speed on deal issues and language. Of course I'm kidding about firing him, there is still plenty to do, but I'm very serious about using a deal attorney.

32. It's ready, set, go – not go, ready, set.

Delays kill deals, so get your financials, contracts, leases and the confidential business review ("the book") ready before launch. You don't want to have to prepare items after a buyer has requested them.

Going to Market

33. Marketing means more than hitting the internet

The world of business buyers is larger than the business-for-sale websites. To get full value, you need to reach out and contact strategic buyers who are not actively searching for businesses to acquire.

34. Don't ignore private equity.

The field of private equity is growing and is even diverting capital from the public markets. Smaller funds are now focused on smaller and mid-sized companies with earnings around $500,000 and up.

35. It is a global market place

We sold a company with their main operations in Brazil to a US based company owned by a UK private equity group. The lead for the buyer came through our European office in the Netherlands. Going to market in many cases means going to the global market.

36. Don't count on finding a stupid buyer.

Stupid buyers exist and will even occasionally make inflated offers to buy a business. Unfortunately, somewhere along the way an attorney, a bank or advisor will show them why an offer doesn't make sense. I've stopped getting excited about crazy offers. They never work. It is far better to have realistic expectations to start with.

37. Send buyers to your M & A advisor.

Buyers will often contact you directly because they don't know you have a representative. Your advisor can save you a lot of time qualifying these buyers and bringing them into the process.

38. Seriously – send buyers to your M & A advisor.

If you get an unsolicited offer (this happens a lot) and don't have an M & A advisor, stop, get an advisor and send the buyer to them. You don't want to negotiate one on one.

39. Get more buyers.

It's a rare buyer who will pay top dollar if they have no competition. Your advisor should be working to get multiple buyers so you can create competition and get your best price.

40. Spit it out.

Disclose negative information early on. It is far better and less disruptive than disclosing it later or during due diligence. Remember that there is no perfect business – they all have negative information.

41. Keep secrets.

You don't need to disclose everything right away. Secrets such as formulas, key customers, and marketing secrets can be left until due diligence.

42. Make them keep secrets.

Get confidentiality agreements from buyers. A buyer shouldn't even know your name without a CA.

43. But don't be paranoid.

There may be a few "bad guys" who you don't want to negotiate with. However, we have had a few sellers who refuse to talk to anyone in their industry because they were afraid to trust them and we were left trying to find buyers in unrelated fields.

44. Ask questions of buyers.

Sometimes you are going to have to carry a note, take an earn-out, etc., so it does matter who you sell to. Ask questions and look for a fit instead of meekly answering questions.

45. Keep the company running.

There is nothing like a drop in sales or earnings to put a deal on hold – possibly forever. It is easy to get distracted during a deal. Use an advisor to minimize the impact on your business and run the process while you keep the company going.

46. Google the buyer.

Multiple times we've had a funny feeling about a buyer, and found them in the worst places on the web, such as ripoffreport.com or in details on court cases. Once, the buyer was fresh out of prison for tax fraud. That doesn't necessarily mean he can't be a good buyer, but it is certainly good information to know.

47. Don't waste your time.

We've seen sellers get approached by a buyer and spend an inordinate amount of time and meetings before ever even knowing what the buyer might pay. Don't do that.

48. Be aware of scams.

There have been acquisition scams. The worst are those in which businesses have been purchased and stripped clean in a week – before the "late" cash payment for the business was made. There are three things to look for: The buyer doesn't ask enough questions, they don't negotiate hard (and thus agree on a high price), and they want to close really fast.

49. Don't tell your employees.

Most buyers don't want to cause undue concern over something that may take many months and may not happen. However, I hate to see an outright lie that may damage trust. If questioned, some fuzzy statement that you are looking for strategic partners or exploring options for growth can do the trick.

50. Tell your employees.

Key employees can help with the sale. For example, the key salesperson may meet with buyers and help them understand the opportunities. Often, your CFO is helpful in completing the deal.

51. Remember your employees.

It is likely that some dedicated employees got you to the point where you could sell your company, so a deal-closing bonus will likely make the post-close period go a lot smoother. You don't want employees feeling like they've been sold down the river.

52. Be consistent.

Buyers, being naturally cautious about the amount of money they could be spending, will ask the same questions over and over again, looking for inconsistencies.

53. Put your money where your mouth is.

If you are expecting big growth and want to be paid for it, be willing to share risk with the buyer. "Trust me, it's going to grow" doesn't work when you tell the buyer that you don't trust them by saying you won't share the risk and take some form of contingent or performance-based payment.

54. Don't get on the emotional roller coaster.

OK, know you will. You will get on the emotional roller coaster. It happens to everyone to some degree. Just know it is coming.

55. Don't get personal.

Hiring an M & A advisor is a way to keep your deal from getting too personal. Although it is wonderful to be able to connect with the buyer on some issues, let your advisor deal with the most contentious ones.

Strategic Buyers

56. Get into their head.

A strategic buyer can boost revenue and/or reduce costs by buying your company (thereby increasing earnings). Research and dig until you have a deep understanding of how they will do this.

57. Show them the money.

Show them you understand where the synergies are, and help show them what revenue/expenses/earnings could be.

58. Don't be ridiculous.

A strategic buyer may pay a premium because of the above, but they will not arbitrarily pay a crazy price just because they want to purchase the company.

59. Sometimes strategic buyers aren't.

We've had "the perfect buyer" come in with a very low offer because they actually know too much about the industry.

Individual Buyers

60. Show me the money.

Some buyers act offended and angry that they should have to show their finances and ability to purchase before being allowed to see confidential information about a company. Tough.

61. Who are they?

Do some research on the buyer. Do they have a resume? References? Criminal record?

62. How to buy a business with no money down.

We see a lot of "buyers" who have all sorts of schemes to buy using reverse mergers, public company shell games and crazy debt-financing schemes. Some of these buyers turn out to be one guy with no money at all. You don't need these guys to overload your company with debt. You could probably manage that on your own.

63. Not so fast.

Many individual buyers want to meet and see the company. There is no need until they have processed all available information and have at least produced a range of values that they would pay.

64. Confidentiality first.

Individual buyers sometimes need to be reminded that they signed a confidentiality agreement. We hate to admit it, but the wife of a prospective buyer once snuck into a retail location to take photos and was caught by the manager. Luckily, that is extremely rare.

65. To SBA or not to SBA.

Some individual buyers will need an SBA loan to finance the purchase. Understand what contingencies are placed on that financing and what it means to you (for example, SBA rules require you to carry a note).

66. Who's on first?

You may have to carry a note, but if another lender is ahead of you, then you will likely have no security on the note. Consider lending the entire amount, and then having the stock, assets and personal guarantee of the buyer as security.

67. Have some empathy.

Most of these buyers are putting practically everything they have in the world on the line to buy your company. That's a good thing to remember when the buyer is getting all worked up about something.

Private Equity Groups (PEGs)

68. Go to their website.

   It isn't foolproof, but a quick check of their website should show what portfolio companies they have and who is on their team. A webpage that says, "Coming soon" means the PEG should soon be answering a lot more questions before you spend much time with them.

69. Show me the money (again).

   Many groups focused on the lower middle market are called, "search funds" or "dry funds" and don't actually have any money. They find businesses, sign LOIs, and then go to investors for the capital. Ask if they can actually write a check, or if they have to go find money. Dry funds are not necessarily bad, but it is important to understand who you are dealing with.

70. Understand the debt structure.

   PEGs will use creative financing structures and it can be important to ask them what financing contingencies will be placed on the deal.

71. Check up on them.

   You hope that the group has a portfolio of companies they have purchased, or some sort of relevant history working with companies. Check them out.

72. Understand the letter of intent.

   Some private equity groups obfuscate the terms on the LOI so it can be hard to figure out just how much cash (and often equity) the seller will end up with. Make sure you understand the basics and ask for clarification if you are confused.

73. Ask again.

   PEGs and intermediaries sometimes speak their own language and may not realize that you didn't understand the explanation you just received. Press them to explain in plain words. It's extremely important and good buyers and M & A advisors understand that it is better to take your time on the LOI.

74. Second bite of the apple.

Rollover equity or buyback of shares in the "newco" can be a wonderful way to get the proverbial second bite of the apple. As we write this, a company we sold 18 months ago has had EBITDA rise by 40 percent this year. The CEO/ex-owner owns 30 percent of the new company and is on his way to matching what he got out of the first deal. Very cool.

Negotiations

75. Competition is the key.

The absolute best way to get the best price is to allow market forces to push the price up.

76. You name the price, I'll name the terms.

Most transactions have a lot of moving parts and it can be difficult to keep them all in perspective. It can be well worth the time to understand all the terms that will define your deal.

77. Don't fixate on cash.

Yes, cash is king. However, sometimes the best deal isn't the one that offers the most cash up front.

78. Refuse earn-outs.

Sometimes there is an over-reliance on earn-outs. If you have a proven, stable company and you have realistic expectations on price, then there is no need to "prove" yourself in the future.

79. Consider earn-outs.

If an earn-out makes sense (typically for a growing company or customer concentration), then you will likely receive substantially less for your company by refusing to consider an earn-out.

80. Be realistic.

I once had clients, a husband and wife team, who absolutely did not want to take a note. They received an offer they would have taken and been happy with, but the price was bid up another $500K – however the $500K was in the form of a note. My clients became agitated and it was difficult to get them to see that no matter what, the offer had not gotten any worse.

81. Take your time.

Keeping things moving is important, but there is no need to rush. For example, is it important to pay attention to offer deadlines? Do you think a serious buyer is going to kill an offer for a multi-million dollar business because of an offer deadline? I've never seen it.

82. Drive the process

We control the timeline and process, instead of letting buyers drive the process. This allows our client to run their business and then review all bids at one time.

The Letter of Intent

83. Speak up!

Have a concern? Speak up, address the issue and, often, the result can be placed in the LOI so all parties will have agreed on how to handle it

84. Bound or unbound?

Most terms of an LOI are non-binding, so arguing too much about why someone may be able to back out is a little silly. However, there are some binding terms such as no-shop/stand-still and confidentiality. Look for them and know what binds you.

85. Non-compete agreement.

You will have to sign one, and the buyer has a right to run the business for some time without worrying about you messing with it after you are gone. However, if you are thinking about competing in a related field, wait until due diligence and have your attorney bring it up. Doing it early just scares the buyer.

86. Work on working capital.

A buyer is going to require working capital (roughly inventory and accounts receivables, less payables) to run the business. In general, for larger deals valued using EBITDA, you will need to deliver the company with enough working capital to run the business. For small companies it is negotiable, and often the seller even keeps and collects "his" accounts receivable. Ask questions and know where you are on this issue.

87. C Corporations require some additional thought

C Corporations can sometimes be a challenge, and it can depend on the assets held, the perceived liabilities of purchasing the company, the customer contracts held and other issues. These issues need to be explored sooner than later with your advisor.

88. Decide whether you want a stock or asset sale.

This can be a ho-hum issue or it could mean the difference between doing the deal and walking away. The issue is basically all about taxes and ongoing liability, so talk to your advisor/CPA/attorney and understand what is going on.

89. Buyers prefer asset sales.

Buyers prefer (and sometimes demand) asset sales because they lower taxes, enhance cash flow, and place past "unknown liabilities" squarely on your shoulders.

90. Lengthy LOI's are OK.

The more you can get worked out at the LOI stage, the smoother the due diligence and definitive document stage will go.

Due Diligence

91. Use an electronic deal room.

The costs have come down substantially for the real data room sites that have watermarks, audit trails, etc., like Firmex, Vrooms and Deal Interactive. If you are creative, you can even use the freebie file sharing sites like Dropbox or box.net to share DD files.

92. Keep your costs down.

Start with the risky, ugly issues that might kill the deal. If they don't, then go ahead and spend more money with the attorney and CPA to finish due diligence.

93. Your attorney works for you.

Some attorneys will "run off with the deal" and run up large fees, especially if you don't proactively give them guidance. So be direct about what you want.

94. Don't hold back.

It all comes out eventually. If you have a dark secret, it's a lot cheaper to disclose and lose the deal than to get sued afterward. It happens. After close, you could spend all that you made on the deal defending yourself in court and no longer have the company.

95. Use your M & A advisor.

It isn't over until it's over. Use your advisor to resolve issues that come up and keep the momentum going.

96. Assign a person to manage the due diligence.

Ideally, you will have an employee (often a controller or office manager) who has been brought in on the fact that you are selling the company. This person can manage the day-to-day processing of the seemingly endless requests for documentation.

97. Keep your eye on the ball.

While you are going through the due diligence process, the buyer will be watching your performance. Make sure that the business is still humming. If you slip, everything will slow down and you start running the risk of losing the deal.

The Close

98. What to do at the close?

Sign.

99. What to do after the close?

Based on some of our clients: More golf, travel with family, travel without family, write a book, start another business, build a home shop to die for, more time with the horses, more time on the boat, more time in the plane, learn to fly and then more time in a new plane.

100. Revisit your financial planner.

OK, we know the truth. You never got one before the deal. But now it is really time to act. New wealth has a lot of traps built in and your planner's job is to keep you out of trouble.

101. Fulfill your obligations.

If you committed to a transition period, work hard for the new owner. Make the transaction successful. It's the right thing to do.

The Author

Ney Grant

Ney Grant has been involved in buying and selling companies for over 25 years. He bought his first company in 1987 and founded a technology company in 1989, which he grew and eventually sold to a public company in 1997. He then served as founder and vice president of acquisitions for a startup that raised $20 million in private equity to fund a series of company acquisitions. Grant executed 11 acquisitions in 18 months with the startup. In addition to serving as Senior M & A advisor to Woodbridge clients, he oversees Woodbridge International's growth on the west coast. He holds an engineering degree from University of California Santa Barbara and an MBA from University of California Davis.

In addition to his business background, Grant is an avid outdoor photographer. He's also a pilot who flies his Cessna around the west coast to visit companies and help get buyers and sellers together. You can visit the Woodbridge website at www.woodbridgegrp.com and visit Grant's personal flying and photography website at www.westcoastflyingadventures.com.

Question or comments? Grant's email address is

ney@woodbridgegrp.com.

Made in the USA
Charleston, SC
03 November 2013